DRINKING WITH DEAD DRUNKS

ELAINE AMBROSE
AK TURNER

Mill Park Publishing
Eagle, Idaho
www.MillParkPublishing.com

Text copyright © 2012 by **Elaine Ambrose** and **AK Turner**

Front cover artwork by **Ward Hooper**

Design and layout by **Blake Beckman, iRockimages.com**

Back cover photograph by **LeAna Earley**

All rights reserved. No parts of this publication may be reproduced, transmitted, or stored without the prior written consent of the publisher.

This is a work of historical fiction. Stories of drinking with Ambrose and Turner, while entertaining and clever, are fiction.

ISBN 978-0-9728225-9-6

Printed in the USA

Mill Park Publishing
Eagle, ID 83616
www.MillParkPublishing.com

"There was no time, in all my waking time, that I didn't want a drink. I began to anticipate the completion of my daily thousand words by taking a drink when only five hundred words were written. It was not long until I prefaced the beginning of the thousand words with a drink."

–Jack London

CONTENTS

Ernest Hemingway
Write Drunk, Edit Sober 9

F. Scott Fitzgerald
Tempest in a Martini Glass 15

Tennessee Williams
Tap Dancing at the Carousel Bar 21

Dylan Thomas
Do Not Go Gentle 27

Hunter S. Thompson
Fear and Loathing with Uncle Duke 33

Jack Kerouac
Love Letters 39

Raymond Chandler
Gimlets and Gumshoes 45

Truman Capote
We're Not in Kansas 51

John Cheever
Letting it Breathe 57

James Joyce
Dogs and Thunder 63

William Faulkner
As I Lay Dying after Four Mint Juleps 69

Frederick Exley
That Long Malaise 75

O. Henry
Satire and Cirrhosis 83

Charles Bukowski
The Mickey Mouse Club 87

Jack London
When the Favorite Haunt Is Haunted 93

Edgar Allan Poe
The Humorist 99

Portraits & Works 105

Introduction

After swilling our way through libations with literary women in *Drinking with Dead Women Writers*, we decided to give the men equal opportunity to belly up to the bar. Surprise! Many male authors were inebriated for much of their adult lives.

Join us as we drink with Ernest Hemingway, F. Scott Fitzgerald, Tennessee Williams, Dylan Thomas, Hunter S. Thompson, Jack Kerouac, Raymond Chandler, Truman Capote, John Cheever, James Joyce, William Faulkner, Frederick Exley, O. Henry, Charles Bukowski, Jack London and Edgar Allan Poe. With beverage in hand, explore the lives, work, and vice of these literary giants.

Cheers,

Elaine and AK

Ernest Hemingway
Write Drunk, Edit Sober

BY ELAINE AMBROSE

I'm eager to meet Ernest Hemingway because we have so much in common. We started our writing careers as journalists, traveled to exotic places around the world, made our homes in Idaho, and we drink too much. There are notable differences between us: He won the Pulitzer Prize and the Nobel Prize for Literature while I have an award medal from Independent Book Publishers and a nice plaque from the Idaho Press Club. And I have no intention of placing a gun into my mouth and pulling the trigger.

I'm sitting on a stone bench at the Ernest Hemingway Memorial along the Big Wood River near Sun Valley. Serene and peaceful, the place rests in vivid contrast to the rugged, handsome author who actively covered several wars, lived in Paris and socialized with Gertrude Stein and James Joyce, survived two plane crashes in Africa, and sailed his boat through the Caribbean in search of giant tuna and marlin. He fascinates me, and I wonder if I can call him Papa.

I hear footsteps on the rock pathway leading from Trail Creek Road. He approaches and stretches out his massive hand, and I'm immediately captivated by his dark mysterious eyes. Those eyes literally charmed the bloomers off of several women including Agnes, Hadley, Pauline, Martha, Mary, and Adriana. I wonder how he found time to write with all the extra dalliances he enjoyed throughout his

DRINKING WITH DEAD DRUNKS

passionate life.

"I have something for you," I say as we sit on the bench. I've rehearsed all week for this occasion but I still need to concentrate to get it correct. I open my cooler and remove a cold silver cocktail shaker, a bottle of Bacardi Rum, a bag of chipped ice, lime juice, and two martini glasses. I notice him smiling as I fill the shaker with ice, add two shots of rum, and cover with one shot of lime juice. Then I shake vigorously until I know the ice and alcohol have reached the perfect blend. I pour the drink into a glass and hand it to him. Delicate ice crystals float on the top of the drink, just as he prefers.

He sips and smiles. "How did you know I don't like sugar in my daiquiri?" he asks.

"You'd be amazed at the information you can find on the Internet," I respond.

He cocks his head as if he wants to ask how that works but changes his mind and takes a long draw while I make myself a daiquiri. Then we clink glasses and he drains his drink while I sip slowly because I want to keep my brain alert enough to finish the interview. I make him a second drink and sense him relaxing.

"Have you ever been to Havana?" he asks, and I realize his only comments have been questions. Just like a journalist.

"No," I respond. "But I suspect it's changed a lot since you lived there."

"Did you read about Constantino at El Flordita Bar?" Another question.

"Yes. He was the famous bartender who made your favorite frozen daiquiri drinks. Sometimes he added grapefruit juice and maraschino liqueur."

Hemingway sets down the drink and stares at me.

"So with this Internet you can instantly access all the information in the world?"

"Well, more information is added every second. And not all of it is correct so you need to research. Many of your biographers wrote conflicting stories about you. But the daiquiri recipe seems to be correct."

He smiles and picks up his drink. I decide to get in a question.

"You were wounded in World War I, reported on the Spanish Civil War, and then received the Bronze Star for bravery during World War II. How did your war experiences influence your writing?"

Hemingway swallows the last of his drink and holds out the empty glass so I prepare another as he talks.

"I drove a Red Cross ambulance during World War I and had an affair with a British nurse, so that became the basis for *A Farewell to Arms*. The brutality I witnessed during the Spanish Civil War inspired *For Whom the Bell Tolls*. By the way, I worked on that novel in Suite 206 of the Sun Valley Lodge, just up the road. But you probably already read about that." He winks at me, and I like it.

We sip our daiquiris and I make another round. He studies the drink and then muses. "This frozen daiquiri, so well beaten as it is, looks like the sea where the wave falls away from the bow of a ship when she is doing thirty knots."

"Isn't that from *Islands in the Stream*?" My facts are getting a bit clouded.

"Yes," he replies. "An intelligent man is sometimes forced to be drunk to spend time with his fools. I drink to make other people more interesting. And I've always said it's best to write drunk and edit sober, but the most essential gift for a good writer is a built-in shockproof, shit detector."

"You wrote that in order to write about life, first you must live it," I respond. "Your life is one of adventure, danger, solitude, literary friends, and women. Can you tell me about your wives and famous friends?"

He laughs out loud and looks beyond us to the west. "Well, Mary, the fourth wife, is buried over there in Ketchum. My grave is beside hers so I guess you could say we've been together the longest. I married my first wife, Hadley, in 1922, and we lived in Paris with a feisty group of writers and artists. Picasso gave me a drawing of a horse and it's hanging in my old home in Havana. I had an intense friendship with F. Scott Fitzgerald, and James Joyce was my best drinking buddy. I was working on *The Sun Also Rises* when I met Pauline. Ah, we had a great time! But Hadley didn't like the affair so she divorced me. I married Pauline in 1927 and we moved to Key West."

He reaches into his pocket, pulls out a long cigar and lights it. He puffs slowly and blows a wispy cloud of smoke toward the monument that holds his bronze bust.

"Damn shame you can't get Cuban cigars here," he says. "Goverment really knows how to destroy a guy's good times. I started going to Cuba during Prohibition and that's where I discovered good rum and the best cigars."

"A true manifestation of manly freedoms," I say. "Weren't you living in a hotel in Havana when you split from Pauline?"

"Yes, indeed." He pauses to remember the facts. "I was having an affair with Martha at the time. We were journalists in Spain and one thing led to another. Pauline and I divorced in 1939 and I married Martha."

"Olé," I say.

"Well, that marriage didn't last long. I met Mary in London and fell madly in love. I divorced Martha and married Mary in 1946. I was determined never to divorce again, even though that darling Adriana in Venice was delicious and tempting. She inspired me to return to Cuba and write *Across the River and into the Trees*."

"One more question," I say with some hesitation. "Why suicide?"

Hemingway finishes the drink and retires the empty glass into the cooler. He stares at the inscription on his memorial. He wrote the eulogy for a friend who died in a hunting accident in Idaho.

> *Best of all he loved the fall*
> *The leaves yellow on cottonwoods*
> *Leaves floating on trout streams*

WRITE DRUNK, EDIT SOBER

And above the hills
The high blue windless skies
Now he will be a part of them forever.

"It's not what they say," he replies. "Sure I was depressed because I feared that I was losing my ability to write. After I wrote *The Old Man and the Sea* in 1951, I said that it was the best I could ever write for all of my life. The book symbolized my belief in victory in defeat, and it won the Pulitzer Prize. I should have been content, but I wasn't. My father, sister and brother all committed suicide. It's because we all suffered from a genetic disease that altered the way our bodies metabolize iron. That disease contributes to mental and physical deterioration. Of course, all those electroconvulsive therapy treatments at the Mayo Clinic in Minnesota didn't help much."

He adds, "But please remember my life, not my death. Ignore my biographers and critics. They write engorged, rambling paragraphs about my restrained, simple writing style. I have the Pulitzer and the Nobel Prize for Literature, and they do not."

He reminds me of Santiago, the old fisherman who battles the giant marlin for three days before he catches it, only to have the great fish eaten by sharks. Hemingway's life proves there is honor in struggle. As he wrote in *The Old Man and the Sea*, "Man is not made for defeat. A man can be destroyed but not defeated."

A cool breeze dances through the aspen leaves as we stand to leave. I pack the cooler and we walk back to Trail Creek Road. He reaches over and takes my hand.

"Remember that there is nothing to writing. All you do is sit down at a typewriter and bleed," he says. "And the first and final thing you have to do in this world is to last it and not be smashed by it."

I am determined to avoid being smashed, and I consider getting sober enough to go fishing.

"Would you like to go to Iconoclast Books in Ketchum?" he asks. "I enjoy visiting there to make sure all my books are on display."

I eagerly nod and try in vain to act nonchalant. "Yes, thank you, Mr. Hemingway."

"Call me Papa."

F. Scott Fitzgerald
Tempest in a Martini Glass

BY AK TURNER

I'm late for my meeting with F. Scott Fitzgerald. We're to meet at The Well in Hollywood, which is supposed to be on Sunset Boulevard, but the entrance is actually on Argyle, so I spend a few minutes looking like a fool before I find it. Scott is already there at a booth in the back. I make my way across a room so dark it seems blackened. I pass by the bar which is an island in the middle of the room. Bottles of liquor are stacked on shelves, in the middle of which sit what appear to be aquariums filled with martini glasses, not delicately ordered, but haphazardly arranged, a chaotic, but artistic tribute to booze.

Scott sits, looking slightly forlorn, less regal than I would have thought, in front of a near-empty martini glass. It may not be his first.

"Their signature drink," he says as I slide in opposite him. "It's called the Hot 'n' Dirty martini. Oh, there she is," he's caught the eye of a waitress and holds his fingers up in a V, signaling for two more. She nods. I guess I'm having a Hot 'n' Dirty martini.

"So, what do you think of this place?" I smile.

He smiles back. "Hollywood is a dump full of the human spirit at a new low of debasement."

I start to panic. There is a difficult evening ahead of me. Before

DRINKING WITH DEAD DRUNKS

I can react to Scott, a woman slides in beside me, forcibly scooting me across the bench of the booth until I'm pressed against the wall.

"What are you doing here?" Scott asks the newcomer.

"Having a drink," replies Zelda Fitzgerald. "Who is she?" She points a finger at me while still staring at Scott.

"She's a reporter," he says, then turns to me. "Is that right? Are you a reporter?" He doesn't wait for me to answer, but turns back to Zelda. "She's a reporter and this is my interview."

"I wish you'd never written *This Side of Paradise*," she says. She's baiting him, but he can't resist.

"Why?"

"Because I never would have married you."

"Perhaps I wish the same," he says.

The waitress arrives and sets the two martinis down in front of the Fitzgeralds. I don't protest, and no one asks what I'd like. The tension overrides all else.

"Ernest was right about you," says Scott.

"Hemingway?" I ask. They ignore me.

"Hemingway was a fairy with hair on his chest," says Zelda.

"This, from the mouth of a failed dancer."

"I could have been a ballerina," she asserts, "but I had you to contend with."

"Only the one book," he taunts. "You're jealous, of course."

"I danced, I painted, I created. All you did was write and drink."

"But I wrote often and well."

"Of course you wrote well, you stole passages from my diary." She turns to me. "He always did believe that plagiarism begins at home."

"I never plagiarized." His voice is calm but his fists are balled.

"Stealing my words wasn't enough," she continues speaking to me. "He also had to alter my work. *My* work. *My* book. He had to interfere and insert his massive importance on my writing."

"*Save Me the Waltz*?" I ask.

"Yes." She smiles sweetly.

TEMPEST IN A MARTINI GLASS

"That wasn't your work, that was my material," hisses Scott.

"It wasn't your material," she snarls back, "it was my life."

"Your life is in an institution; leave me to my interview."

"Who is the jealous one? I think you're angry that I published *Save Me the Waltz* before you finished *Tender Is the Night*."

"I have to think," I interject, "that between the two of you, there was enough material in your marriage for you both to write about it." I'm thinking out loud and they each respond to my comment with hostile eyes.

"Wait," says Scott, addressing Zelda, "Are you still alive? Or are you here like I am?"

"No," she says, and now they speak to each other with kindness. "I died eight years after you."

"How?" He reaches for her hand.

"There was a fire in the hospital."

"At Sheppard Pratt in Baltimore?"

"No. Remember, I went to Highland Mental Hospital in Asheville after that."

"Oh, yes. I do remember."

"I was locked in a room, waiting for my electroshock therapy."

"I'm so sorry."

"Remember the last time we saw each other?" asks Zelda. I debate giving them privacy, but their tenderness is fleeting.

"How could I not? That disastrous trip to Cuba." He frowns.

"You were a drunken mess."

"And you were insane," he counters.

"I'll leave you to your interview now." Zelda stands and addresses me. "Don't bother peeling him off the floor, just leave him where he falls." She disappears into the dark of the bar.

The martini glasses are empty and the waitress approaches.

"Would you like another?" she asks Scott. He nods. "And would you like a drink?" she asks, seeing me for the first time. I emerge from the corner of the booth where Zelda had crushed me against the wall and reclaim my place opposite Scott.

DRINKING WITH DEAD DRUNKS

"Yes. I definitely want a drink. I'll try the Rumba Punch."

The waitress leaves and I turn back to Scott, who has the same forlorn look he wore when I first found him.

"You seem wounded by her," I say.

"Who, Zelda? She's not a wound, she's more like a split in the skin that won't heal because there's not enough material."

"I didn't expect her here. I want you to know that was as much of a surprise to me as it was to you."

"A great social success is a pretty girl who plays her cards as though she were plain. Zelda could never be plain, could not even pretend."

"She's fiery," I say, meaning it as a compliment.

"That's the best thing a girl can be in this world," he says, "a beautiful little fool."

I don't like this comment and want to take issue, but the drinks arrive and I'm desperate to put a haze on the evening. Scott changes the subject for me.

"We were beautiful and we were damned, but let's not talk of Zelda further. I like people and I like them to like me, but I wear my heart where God put it, on the inside."

"Suits me," I say. "Let's talk about writing. It can be kind of a lonely life, no?"

"Yes, but it's also the cure for loneliness."

"How so?"

"That is part of the beauty of all literature. You discover that your longings are universal longings, that you're not lonely and isolated from anyone. You belong."

"Yes, I agree that as a reader you can feel less lonely, realizing that others feel the same, but when you're writing, it's still lonely as hell."

"We'll always have this to keep us company." He raises his Hot 'n' Dirty martini and I meet it with my Rumba Punch.

"*The Great Gatsby* was reprinted after your death and has long been considered a literary classic. Another movie is in the works now."

Scott smiles but then adds, "I regret the title, it's only fair."

"Are you kidding? The title is fantastic."

"I wanted to call it *Trimalchio in West Egg*."

I grimace. "I have to say, I'm really glad you went with *The Great Gatsby*."

"She had something to do with that." He nods in the direction of his departed wife. "And my editor."

"Well, you may be a literary great, but I'm not taking your advice when it comes to titles. What other advice do you have regarding writing?"

"The world only exists in your eyes. You can make it as big or as small as you want."

"I like that. And it's true."

"And for God's sake, cut out all the exclamation points. An exclamation point is like laughing at your own joke. It's nothing but a sad little cheat that writers employ."

"Noted." I frown, contemplating my guilt. "When did you start writing?"

"When I was very young, as soon as I could. I wrote a detective story when I was thirteen."

"I would have loved to have read that."

"They published it in the school paper."

"It seems a fitting start."

"It was. Of course, three years later I was booted from school as not much of a student. That's also somehow fitting, I suppose."

"I'm pretty sure you're not the first, nor the last writer to be kicked out of school."

The earlier melancholy has returned, though I can't fathom that he's actually saddened by recalling an expulsion at the age of sixteen. I flag down the waitress, different from our earlier server. She approaches our table.

"I was just looking for our waitress," I say.

"Bernice is off now, but I'm Daisy. I can take your order."

DRINKING WITH DEAD DRUNKS

"Okay, we'll have one more Hot 'n' Dirty and one more Rumba."

"I'll have those for you in just a minute," she says.

I turn back to Scott. "You know, a lot of writers look to you as their hero."

"Show me a hero, and I'll write you a tragedy."

"Still, you were better than you ever knew."

Daisy arrives with the next round and we turn our attention to our drinks. Fitzgerald doesn't want to be cheered or lauded, he wants to focus on his Hot 'n' Dirty martini. I'll allow him this, because the evening has been more eventful than I could have hoped. And I'm digging the Rumba Punch. After a moment, Scott breaks the stillness and silence and raises his glass.

"A toast," he proposes.

"A toast," I agree.

"To alcohol, the rose-colored glasses of life."

Tennessee Williams
Tap Dancing at the Carousel Bar

BY ELAINE AMBROSE

I stifle a giddy laugh as I walk into the Carousel Bar in the historic Hotel Monteleone in the French Quarter of New Orleans. The glittering circular bar with twenty-five hand-painted seats rotates every fifteen minutes and offers one of the world's best cocktail experiences. Since 1949, the Carousel Bar has inspired stories, television programs, books, and artists. Hemingway, Faulkner, and Capote are just a few of the famous authors who were regular patrons. And it's a favorite place of the incomparable playwright and author Tennessee Williams.

I join him at a private table next to a big window overlooking Royal Street. He seems melancholy at first but then his mood changes to almost perky optimism as I introduce myself. The table is covered with an intriguing array of unique appetizers.

"I can't wait for you to try some of the Carousel Bar delicacies," he gushes. "I've ordered the Artisan Pizzette special. This one is oyster and artichoke, and this one is eggplant caviar with barbecued shrimp, and here are some antipasti with smoked goat cheese. Really, you *must* share with me."

I thank him and then sample one of the appetizers.

"This certainly is different from the Tater Tots and catsup we have back in Idaho," I say.

DRINKING WITH DEAD DRUNKS

"Oh, here," he points with enthusiasm. "Try the red bean and boudin sausage. It's divine!"

I do as instructed and savor the moment and the flavor. A dark-skinned, exotic woman delivers our drinks and quietly leaves. I look at the mysterious drinks and then stare at Williams for the description.

"This is the specialty of the Carousel Bar," he says with great pride. "It's called a Vieux Carre Cocktail, and it's a delightful blend of Benedictine liqueur, Peychaud and Angostura bitters, rye whiskey, cognac and dry vermouth. *Vieux Carré* is the title of a play I wrote here in 1977. This drink is guaranteed to knock you on your butt!"

I take a sip and catch my breath. If I blew on a lit candle, it would ignite a fireball.

"Very tasty," I gasp.

Williams opens a pill bottle, removes an assortment of colorful capsules, and downs them with a long swallow. His eyes close and I fiddle with a shrimp until he returns to reality.

"Welcome to New Orleans," he says. "I'm Tennessee Williams."

"Thank you, Mr. Williams. I appreciate your time, and I'm so excited to be here. Didn't you refer to this bar in *A Streetcar Named Desire*?"

"Ah, yes I did," he answers. "The Carousel atmosphere is magical. And as I wrote in the play, I don't want realism. I want magic!"

"I think there's magic in theatre. You won the Pulitzer Prize for Drama for both *A Streetcar Named Desire* and *Cat on a Hot Tin Roof*. Both plays became successful motion pictures. Were they your greatest achievements?"

His ebullient demeanor instantly sours. I try desperately to rephrase the question and change the dark mood.

"I mean, your writing is so vivid and powerful," I say. "I'm sure you are pleased with your many successes."

He takes another long drink and then smiles. I am relieved. We break the tension by attacking the eggplant caviar.

TAP DANCING AT THE CAROUSEL BAR

"It's all such a dilemma," he says. "My successes came as a result of my pain and failures. You see why this is so traumatic?"

I nod and sip my drink. The rotating bar is getting on my nerves.

"I had a nervous breakdown when I was twenty-four and quit my job. Then the only employment I could get was as a factory worker. That menial work inspired the character of Stanley Kowalski in *Streetcar*. My father was an abusive drunk who beat me because I was effeminate. Back in the 1930s, fathers did that to their homosexual sons."

"I think we're more enlightened now," I offer as encouragement.

"Yes," he answers. "About time."

"I know you were close to your sister Rose. Didn't she inspire the character of Laura, the disabled girl in *The Glass Menagerie*?"

"True. My dear Rose was so delicate and frail. We were only sixteen months apart and we survived our abusive and domineering parents by protecting each other. Yes, Rose is Laura."

"*The Glass Menagerie* became one of seven plays to be made into a major motion picture. Were you satisfied with the screen adaptations?"

Williams finishes his cocktail and motions for two more. Another gorgeous woman appears, statuesque and mysterious with bright white eyes and a slight smile. She leaves our drinks and then disappears behind the Carousel Bar. I take a sip that sets my mouth on fire; I soothe it with goat cheese.

"The movies were fine because of directors such as Elia Kazan and stars such as Marlon Brando, Vivien Leigh, Elizabeth Taylor, and Paul Newman. They all did outstanding jobs of portraying mental instability and alcoholism. It's as if they lived my life."

"At least your experiences made movies that live on after you're gone."

"As I wrote in *Sweet Bird of Youth*, I can't expose a human weakness on the stage unless I know it through having it myself."

I notice that he's about to go dark again so I change the subject. "Your name was Thomas Lanier Williams III. Why change it to

DRINKING WITH DEAD DRUNKS

Tennessee?"

"Well, I came from Tennessee ancestors," he answers. "And don't you think that Tennessee is more literary than Tom?" He winks, and I'm relieved that he is in a good mood again.

"I've read that you traveled and moved often to learn about other cultures and personalities that you could incorporate into your plays and stories."

"I spent many summers in Europe. I lived in New York, New Orleans, Key West, Rome, Barcelona, and London. I was driven to find another place, another source of inspiration. All this happened during the years of my best work. And Frank Merlo was with me."

He's instantly somber and slumps in his chair. I know that their relationship lasted fourteen years before Merlo died from lung cancer, and I frantically turn the conversation.

"You are recognized and appreciated around the world," I say, feeling like a tap dancer. "There is the Tennessee Williams Theatre in Key West. And you've been inducted into the Poets' Corner at the Cathedral Church of Saint John the Divine. And the Tennessee Williams Literary Festival is organized every year right here in New Orleans."

He washes down more pills with the rest of his drink. "In *The Milk Train Doesn't Stop Here Anymore*, I write that we all live in a house on fire, no fire department to call; no way out, just the upstairs window to look out of while the fire burns the house down with us trapped, locked in it."

At this point, I consider asking for some of his pills. But I shake the urge and finish my drink. I think the interview is over so I start to reach for my briefcase.

"Wait!" His eyes open wide and he grins with alarming delight. He is noticeably jolly. "You can't leave until you try the Golden Cadillac!"

I'm hesitant to ask so he tells me.

"It's a fabulous drink made from Galliano, light Creme de Cacao and Half and Half. It's a house specialty and the perfect way to end

TAP DANCING AT THE CAROUSEL BAR

our glorious conversation!"

Yes, I think to myself. He's nuts.

Before I can object, he orders the drinks and another stunning woman floats over with a silver tray. She must be over six feet tall and a split in her silver gown reveals the longest legs I've ever seen. At this point, I'm feeling a bit intimidated in my sandals, cropped khakis and "I Love Jazz" t-shirt, but she smiles warmly at me, removes the empty plates and glasses, and retreats.

Williams and I clink. I must admit, this is a damn good cocktail. Smooth and creamy with a hint of sweet brandy. The Carousel Bar rotates, the musicians play rhythmic jazz music, and I smile because for a brief moment in time, Tennessee Williams is content.

DRINKING WITH DEAD DRUNKS

Dylan Thomas
Do Not Go Gentle

BY AK TURNER

We're illuminated by the red neon of the White Horse Tavern. The light shines off slick pavement on the corner of Hudson and 11th in Manhattan. I'm trying to gently shuffle Dylan Thomas off to the side, because as it is, we're on display. He can't be moved, though, doubled over and retching uncontrollably.

I can't say I didn't foresee this as a possibility, but I thought this might be how we'd end the night, not begin it. And he's neither vomiting, nor drunk, but consumed by this violent fit of coughing. An under-aged gaggle of girls crosses the street to avoid us. Dylan's hacking echoes through every alley in Manhattan. Abruptly, he stops.

"You're not tubercular, too, are you?" he asks. I shake my head. "Oh, good." He doubles over and begins again, ending only when a spatter of red appears on the street.

"Blood!" he cries. "That's the stuff." He wipes the corners of his mouth where blood and saliva have mixed into a ghoulish lipstick. "Now that's done, shall we have a drink?"

I am not tall by any means, a hair under 5'4". But Dylan Thomas may actually be shorter than I am. We're at a level gaze, but he's got thick heels on his shoes and I'm in flats.

"Sure," I say. "Let's have a drink. As long as you're all right."

DRINKING WITH DEAD DRUNKS

"It can't get any worse."

We enter the White Horse and sit at a small round table, the type you might find in any bar, anywhere in the world. As if allergic to the chair, Dylan pops back up instantly, his curls bobbing as he does so.

"What can I get you to drink, will you have a whiskey? We'll have beer first and whiskey later? I'll just tell them to keep it coming, yes?"

I open my mouth to respond but he's already gone, delivering instructions to the bartender, a tall, skinny and bald man, a physical foil to Dylan.

"I've got about eight different Dylans in me," he says upon his return with two pints of beer. "Which Dylan do you want?"

"I don't know," I answer. "What are my options?"

"Well, there's the sickly one, to start, but you've already seen him, so I'll do my best to give you a sampling of the rest of me." He pulls an inhaler from his pocket, uses it, and takes a sip of his beer. This is a practiced move, I can tell. One hand on the inhaler, one on the drink. He reeks of cigarettes.

"You have a beautiful voice," I offer. "I see why you loved to read your work aloud, and why people wanted to listen to you."

"Thank you. I did hundreds of recordings for the BBC with this voice. It's my second greatest attribute."

"What's the first?"

He leans in close and looks me dead on. He raises an eyebrow, then freezes in this pose and with this expression. I'm not sure whether to laugh or run. Then he abruptly sits back in his chair and smiles big. "The words themselves, of course." He laughs, the intensity of the previous minute gone. "I discovered words, the way we all do as children through stories, and I fell in love."

"I'll drink to that," I say.

"Cheers, my dear." He raises his pint. We clink. We drink. It's a dark beer, but easy on the hops. I don't ask him the specifics of it. "You know what I'd love?" He pauses, bringing his inhaler again to his lips. His lungs inflate leaving him just as short, but twice as stout. "I'd love a sweet of some sort! A custard or cream or tart of some kind. I've got a craving."

"I guess this will just have to do," I say, raising my glass.

"Yes, yes," he says, but as I drink, he sets his beer down. His mind is stuck on the longing for sugar and I realize I'm out-drinking him, which is unexpected. He darts up from his chair. "I'm going to smoke. I'll return in a moment."

As he walks to the door I notice his butt. I'm not trying to look at his butt, but I can't help it. It's… substantial. As he reaches the doorway, I see that his left hand holds his inhaler, and his right wields an already-lit cigarette.

"Okay, then," I mutter to myself and finish my beer. Then I finish his beer. I approach the bar. "I'll have two more of whatever these were." As the pale, slight bartender pours, I steal a peek outside. I see Dylan using the stub of his first cigarette to light a second. I return to our table and set to drinking. That's what we're supposedly here to do, after all.

I'm halfway through my fresh pint when I hear the hacking. "Oh, no." I creep up to the window and sure enough, Dylan Thomas is again in a fit of retching, though he's taking advantage of every pause in the hacking to alternately employ his inhaler or take a drag from his smoke. I go back to the table and finish my beer. Maybe this makes me unkind, but he is dead, after all, so it's not as if he can be in any mortal danger. The hacking fit dies down. I see him turn toward the door, then stop for one more pull of the inhaler. Before he reaches our table, I've poured half of his beer into my glass, so that our pints appear in a similar state as they had upon his departure.

He sits and smiles at me.

"Are you all right?" I ask.

"Of course I'm all right. Are we ready for whiskey then?" He drinks his beer and once again shoots up out of his chair. "Bartender, we'll have two more pints and four whiskeys, please."

"*Four* whiskeys?" I protest, but I don't get up.

DRINKING WITH DEAD DRUNKS

Dylan Thomas turns back to me. "We're here to drink, are we not?" Our table is only a few steps away from the bar, so I remain seated and let Dylan make the three short trips with the drinks. He places the pints on my side of the table, and all four shots of whiskey on his, which suits me just fine.

"All right, then. Cheers." I raise my beer to his shot.

"I've got something to show you," he says, and scoots his chair around so that we're side by side. There is an odor to him, something more than just nicotine. Tiny veins stretch on and around his bulbous nose. He removes a worn newspaper clipping from his wallet. "Look, here's me, I won the 220-yard dash when I was twelve. They put my picture in the paper."

"That's wonderful," I say, because I can tell that this is somehow important to him.

"I can see the boys of summer in their ruin…" he touches the clipping.

"What else do you have in there?" I ask, gesturing to his wallet.

"Not a thing." He flexes his wallet so that I can see inside the empty folds. As a patron leaves, a gust of wind comes to us from the street outside. "Can you smell that rain? It'll be tough lungs today."

I want to talk more about the newspaper clipping, but he carefully folds it and returns it to the confines of the limp wallet. Of all the press he received in his life, this is what he carries with him.

"Do you have any regrets about all of this?" I ask.

"All of what?"

"The bar, the alcohol, your writing, the adult you versus the twelve-year-old who won that race?"

"No, I don't regret any of it. I'm not capable of that sort of thing. I am poet and drink and meteors and voice." He's grown suddenly louder. He finishes his first whiskey and takes a drink of the second. "And all I can do is rage!"

Up until now he hasn't consumed that much alcohol, relative to what I'd expected. But that changes. He finishes the second whiskey, drinks the third and fourth in quick succession. He gets up from his chair, though slower now than his earlier explosions. "I'm having four more whiskeys," he states. "Would you like two more pints?"

"Yes," I admit.

"Good girl."

We shuffle back and forth between the bar and our table, returning empty glasses in exchange for full ones. Settled again with ridiculous amounts of alcohol before us, Dylan precisely lines up his four shot glasses.

"All right," he says. "You have to come up with a toast for each of these. What's this first one for?"

"To Dylan Thomas!"

"That's very sweet." He smiles, "To Dylan Thomas."

He drinks the whiskey, I sip my beer.

"And this one?" He holds up number two and I realize there won't be any breaks.

"To *Portrait of the Artist as a Young Dog*."

"To *Portrait of the Artist as a Young Dog*," he agrees. We drink. He looks at me expectantly.

"Oh, right." I raise my beer again. "To *A Child's Christmas in Wales*."

"To *A Child's Christmas in Wales*." We drink again. "And the last?" he asks.

"To *Silkwood*."

"To *what*?" He holds his final shot in midair.

"Oh, wait, no, not the movie," I correct myself. "To *Under Silkwood*."

He sets down his whiskey, purses his lips and narrows his eyes.

"No, that's not right." My brain is scrambling but I just can't get it. All I can see are Meryl Streep and Kurt Russell. Then it hits me. "To *Under Milk Wood*," I yell triumphantly.

"To *Under Milk Wood*," he says with calm. "You had me alarmed there for a minute."

"Sorry." I smile.

"I have to go cough up some blood and maybe have a cigarette," he says. "Would you mind settling up here for us?"

"Of course," I say. "I'll meet you outside." I finish the last of my beer and fumble with cash, dropping bills. I look to the bartender with embarrassment. There is no judgment in his eyes.

On the sidewalk, Dylan is once again in the throes of coughing, smoking, and using his inhaler.

"This has been lovely," I call loudly over the sound of retching.

Dylan nods his agreement, unable to speak while battling for breath. I pat him on the back and see Hunter S. Thompson walk by, enter the White Horse, and sit at the very table we left. My attention returns to Dylan, now standing erect and gaining composure, though his earlier energy has been sodden by whiskey.

"All is well and not to worry," he says. "Death shall have no dominion."

Hunter S. Thompson
Fear and Loathing with Uncle Duke

BY ELAINE AMBROSE

How to get energized for an interview with an alcoholic, suicidal writer whose major works include the words fear, loathing, curse, and hell in the titles? I wisely decide to avoid wearing the perky party dress and pearls and choose the Bohemian skirt, t-shirt and vest. Knowing that Hunter S. Thompson had been a fan of firearms, I bring along my concealed weapon permit to show him, just in case.

We're meeting at the White Horse Tavern in the Greenwich Village area of Manhattan, one of Thompson's favorite pubs. I enter the tavern just as a disheveled man reeking of whiskey and cigarettes stumbles out the door. He resembles Dylan Thomas but I disregard the coincidence because I know he's dead.

I recognize Thompson sitting at a table next to the bar and I approach to introduce myself. He slowly sips his rum and then motions for me to sit. Bob the bartender calls for my order so I request a Lager Shandy, a drink made of beer and lemonade. He brings the drink and abruptly tosses down a bowl half filled with broken nuts and stale pretzels.

"Cash only," Bob mutters. I fumble for money and then ask if we can start a tab. Bob snorts and replies. "Maybe, if you skip the lemonade."

DRINKING WITH DEAD DRUNKS

So far I'm not impressed with the service at the White Horse Tavern. I hand him a ten spot and say that we'll pay as we go. Bob snatches the money and skulks back to his station behind the bar.

Thompson watches the exchange with detached amusement. "Ol' Bob's been here forever and he's not fond of the Shandy," he says. "As I once wrote, 'Good people drink good beer.'"

"I'll keep that in mind," I answer and then take a drink. The lemonade is as sour as Bob's service. The awkward silence is broken when Thompson drains his rum and slams down the glass. Bob appears instantly with another rum cocktail.

"It's on the house, Mr. Thompson." Bob doesn't seem surprised by Thompson's return from the grave, which I attribute to age, alcohol, or simply a lack of information. Perhaps he never heard the news.

I decide to humor Bob because I know from vast experience that it's never wise to annoy the bartender. "I'll take a Black and Tan next." He instantly grins and nods his head, obviously pleased that I've matured past the lemonade.

"Finally an excellent choice! And I'll let you run a tab."

We're all pleased that I have learned the ordering protocol at the White Horse. Rum and beers continue to flow, without lemonade, and the mood is momentarily jolly.

"Thanks for meeting me today," I say. "I'm interested in your writing style. A *New York Times* reviewer once praised you as a spirited, witty, observant and original writer."

"That was for my book about the Hell's Angels motorcycle gang. After it was published, some dirty bikers beat the crap out of me because I wouldn't share profits from the book. But it turned out just fine because Random House used the fight to promote the book."

"Didn't you get high with the Angels?" I ask, knowing the answer.

Thompson shares a tired smile.

"I've tried it all – dope, heroin, speed, acid, and cocktails of a combination of illegal substances that should have killed me. The

FEAR AND LOATHING WITH UNCLE DUKE

hallucinations are bad, but after awhile you learn to cope with things like seeing your dead grandmother crawling up your leg with a knife in her teeth. Most acid fanciers can handle this sort of thing."

I cringe at the grandmother vision. Then he tries to justify his drug usage.

"I support the legalization of drugs because that's the only way to deal with them. Look at Prohibition; all it did was make a lot of criminals rich."

I finish the Shandy as Bob brings the Black and Tan, proudly revealing an expert balance of light pale ale and stout Guinness. It leaves a frothy rim on my lip. Thompson orders another cocktail.

"Speaking about drugs," he says, "I haven't found a drug yet that can get you anywhere near as high as sitting at a desk writing."

"We're in agreement there," I say. "And I know you developed Gonzo journalism while writing for *Rolling Stone* magazine."

"All I do is write articles in first person and add some humor or bizarre anecdotes to make it more interesting. I attempt to tell the truth but sometimes use exaggeration. Oh, hell, I lie all the time."

He chuckles and we sip our drinks.

"I wrote with the Gonzo method in *Fear and Loathing in Las Vegas*. It's just a clever technique to jump into the story as a journalist in Vegas with two bags full of grass, acid, cocaine, uppers, downers, and a quart of rum. See how it works? I get to write stories and include all my vices as props for the plot."

"I've never tried that approach," I lie. Suddenly I see images of friends scoffing at that. *Sure,* they clamor in my head, *as if you never use drinking as a theme.* I shoo them away and focus again as Thompson speaks.

"Well, I hate to advocate drugs, alcohol, violence, or insanity to anyone, but they've always worked for me."

"Nice quote," I say.

"Should be a bumper sticker," he answers.

"You started your writing career in high school, even though you didn't finish because of that unfortunate incident that sent you to jail before graduation."

"Yes," he agreed. "I always seem to get on the wrong side of the law. But you're correct. At an early age I wrote that I was going to be a writer. I said I'm not sure if I'll be a good one or even a self-supporting one, but until the dark thumb of fate pressed me to the dust and says 'you are nothing', I will be a writer. Besides, I have no taste for either poverty or honest labor, so writing is the only recourse left for me."

"I've read that you used a typewriter to copy the works of F. Scott Fitzgerald and Ernest Hemingway to learn how they wrote. Did that help?"

"Of course it did. I was so fascinated by Hemingway that I traveled to Ketchum, Idaho to investigate and write about his suicide back in 1961. Now I feel badly about stealing those elk antlers that were hanging above the front door of his cabin. Probably shouldn't have done that."

"Probably not."

"But I defend an artist's right to know and study influential mentors. For example, Johnny Depp played the starring role in *Fear and Loathing in Las Vegas*. He lived with me in order to learn how to correctly play the role. He also starred in the film adaptation of *The Rum Diary*. We're still friends. Now, speaking of rum…"

Thompson downs his drink and raises the glass toward the bar. Bob hurries over with two more drinks. My Black and Tan looks a bit fuzzy but I concentrate as Thompson explains more of his maverick philosophy. I nibble on the pretzels and nuts in a feeble attempt to get sober.

"Life should not be a journey to the grave with the intention of arriving safely in a pretty and well-preserved body, but rather to skid in broadside in a cloud of smoke, thoroughly used up, totally worn out, and loudly proclaiming 'Wow! What a ride!'"

We touch glasses in mutual approval.

"Another thing," Hunter Thompson is slightly inebriated and I sense another speech. "We are all alone, born alone, die alone, and

FEAR AND LOATHING WITH UNCLE DUKE

– in spite of *True Romance* magazines – we shall all someday look back on our lives and see that, in spite of our company, we were alone the whole way. I do not say lonely – at least, not all the time – but essentially, and finally, alone. This is what makes your self-respect so important, and I don't see how you can respect yourself if you must look in the hearts and minds of others for your happiness."

This soliloquy elicits another clink. Then he frowns.

"We are turning into a nation of whimpering slaves to Fear—fear of war, fear of poverty, fear of random terrorism, fear of getting down-sized or fired because of the plunging economy, fear of getting evicted for bad debts or suddenly getting locked up in a military detention camp on vague charges of being a terrorist sympathizer."

"Damn," I mutter. "I'm still in the happiness mode and you've ruined it with all this talk about fear."

"Never turn your back on fear. It should always be in front of you, like a thing that might have to be killed," he says solemnly. "The highways are crowded with people who drive as if their sole purpose in getting behind the wheel is to avenge every wrong done them by man, beast or fate. The only thing that keeps them in line is their fear of death, jail and lawsuits."

He pauses, closes his eyes, and rubs his bald head. I wonder if he's having a flashback. I peek under the table and expect to see his grandmother creeping up his leg with her trusty knife. Then he's back, eyes wide open, waxing philosophically.

"So we shall let the reader answer this question for himself: Who is the happier man, he who has braved the storm of life and lived or he who has stayed securely on shore and merely existed?"

"Hunter," I moan. "You're making my brain hurt. I just want to know what makes you such a complicated writer."

"Life has become immeasurably better since I have been forced to stop taking it seriously."

I recognize his quote, and we smile.

"This interview reminds me of your 2004 documentary titled *Come on Down: Searching for the American Dream*. You interviewed director Adamm Liley over drinks in a tavern."

"Don't follow my example," he says. "I shot myself the following year."

"Yes, it seems odd that you would commit suicide with your son, daughter-in-law and grandchild in the house and your wife on the phone. I know you're a firearms and explosive enthusiast, but why shoot yourself?"

"Well, when the truth becomes dull and depressing, the only working alternative is wild bursts of madness and filigree," he says. "I would feel trapped in this life if I didn't know I could commit suicide at any time. On my tombstone, I wanted them to carve that it never got fast enough for me."

"At least you live on as the character of Uncle Duke in the *Doonesbury* comic strip."

"Sure do," he says. "I was irritated about that at first and threatened to set fire to Garry Trudeau, the cartoonist. But then I got to like it. I should be remembered as a cartoon."

We finish our drinks and Bob brings the bill, astute enough to know not to bring more drinks. I pull out the necessary money and anchor it to the table with the empty peanut bowl.

Thompson says as we stand to leave, "At my funeral, my ashes were shot from a cannon to the sounds of 'Spirit in the Sky,' and there were multi-colored fireworks and famous dignitaries. As I've always said, *Res ipsa loquitur*. Let the good times roll."

Jack Kerouac
Love Letters

BY AK TURNER

In pictures of the younger Kerouac, I thought him quite handsome. He always looked so self-assured. But this is not the younger Kerouac. His face is puffy and he's undeniably nervous, fidgeting with hands and feet, unable to keep his gaze from roaming. We're at the White Horse in Manhattan, where I'm strangely becoming a regular, and I think his demeanor has more to do with the place than with me. He's laughed and fought and cried and been thrown out of this bar. I'm told that the men's room wall reads with the clear graffiti, "Go home, Jack." I decide it's not worth it to see for myself.

"You know," I say, "you don't need to be nervous, the people here don't know you."

"Yeah, that's the trouble," answers Kerouac. "That's always the trouble."

"Why don't we have a drink?"

"I drink whiskey."

I leave our small table, approach Bob at the bar and order a whiskey and a Hefeweizen. When I return, Jack looks no calmer, but begins sipping his drink. It is immediately apparent that he's not going to speak unless I pose a direct question.

"So, do you want to talk about the Beat Generation?" I ask.

DRINKING WITH DEAD DRUNKS

"I do not want to talk about the Beat Generation." He's quiet and studies the table.

"Oh, I'm sorry."

He drinks. I wait. Minutes pass. His drink is empty so I go to the bar and get him another. He drinks this, then looks at me squarely. "I don't like the title 'Father of the Beat Generation', so I tell people that. I tell them that I don't like that, I don't like them calling me that. And what do they do? They introduce me as: Jack Kerouac, who doesn't like the title 'Father of the Beat Generation.' That make sense to you?"

"I can see why that would bother you," I say.

"It's not my fault that certain Bohemian elements might have found something in my writing to hang their beatnik theories on."

He shuts down again, back to nerves and doubt, and I realize that the only way I'm going to get more of the glib Kerouac I'm hoping for is if he's drunk. I return to the bar and order one more Hefeweizen and two more whiskeys. It takes twenty minutes of silence and drinking before a new Kerouac begins to show his teeth.

The silence is broken when he says something in French, which I don't speak.

"I'm sorry?" I ask.

He waves me off. "What do you want to know? What are we here for? Books, God, death, what are we talking about?"

"You know, your voice is not what I'd imagined." This is my way of saying that he sounds like a thug. "But I guess we should start with *On the Road*."

"I just wrote what I saw. And I believed in what I saw and in the loneliness of my life. We're all going to die."

The social oddities of Jack Kerouac may change with drink, but they will not depart.

"I read somewhere that you wrote on teletype paper, on one long continuous roll of paper so you wouldn't have to pause to insert new sheets into a typewriter."

"Yeah. For the type of writing I do, that's better. Better for a narrative."

"Will you tell me about some of your influences?"

"Sure, my influences. Jazz is one. And Buddhism."

"But what about other writers?"

"Other writers, sure. Joyce, Melville, Wolfe."

"Tell me about Lucien."

"Carr? You want to know about Lucien Carr?" he smiles. "Talented, funny. Drew people to him. They couldn't help themselves. He was like the sun."

"I guess so."

"What's that supposed to mean?"

"I read about the killing of David Kammerer."

"Lucien did what he had to do in self-defense. Anyone who knew Carr or Kammerer knows that's the honest truth."

"Do you think Kammerer was in love with Carr?"

"It wasn't love. It was obsession the size of the universe."

"And you helped him dump the body in the Hudson, right?"

"No, I never dumped a body in the Hudson," Jack looks briefly aghast. "I just helped him get rid of the knife, is all." He's on his fourth whiskey and close to sauced.

"You spent some time in jail for that."

"Only because my father wouldn't bail me. That's all right. I called Edie Parker, she was a girlfriend at the time. Her family bailed me out if I'd marry her."

"Did you?"

"Yeah."

"How'd that go?"

"We had it annulled within a year."

"All of this must have had quite an impact on your writing," I say, which sounds moronic, but I've already blurted it out.

"Yeah, it had an impact. But when I was four, my older brother died. You want impact? There you go."

"Tell me—"

"He was my guardian angel, my brother was. Followed me

through my whole life. What did you ask me?"

"I–"

"But back to Lucien, he was a wonderful person. There were so many. Neal and Lucien both. Neal was pure life exploding into a million blue spiders, just crawling across the sky." His speech takes on a slur.

"Can I ask about–"

"I've got millions of true stories in my head. Millions. Don't tell nobody. Promise you won't tell nobody? There are millions."

I'm quiet, waiting for more.

"Aren't you gonna ask me another question?" he asks.

"Are you going to let me?"

"Of course I'll let you. Ask me anything you want. Go ahead."

"I wanted to ask–"

"We were talking about Buddhism before. If you want to know more about that, read *Desolation Angels*. That's more the end of my Buddhism than the beginning. And all the early stuff is way too Catholic. I was a fire lookout. Did you know that? I was a fire lookout, I was Merchant Marine, I was Navy."

He looks up at me suddenly, as if I'm new to our table of two.

"Did you want to ask me something?"

"Sure, I'll try. If you hadn't been a writer, what would you have done?"

"Mailman," he says without missing a beat. He turns then from our tiny table to stare at the back of one of the patrons at the bar. He is intense and focused. "That guy," he mutters.

"Do you know him?" I whisper.

"No, but he doesn't like me." He's gritting his teeth. The man in question is unaware of our presence, but I recognize in Kerouac what I've seen before from committed drinkers. It's the fabrication of hostility to reach the goal of bar fight. Kerouac's faux foe is rough around the edges, but youthful, a man who hasn't yet seen the far side of thirty, and he looks as if he's spent a long day working with his hands.

LOVE LETTERS

"No, no, no," I say. "Listen to me. That guy is fine. He doesn't know you, he hasn't even seen you, and I'm not too keen on being in the middle of a brawl. Jack?" He's still staring at the back of a worn Carhartt. "Jack!"

"What?" He turns to me, startled.

"Listen to me. Let it go. Just calm down and let it go."

He looks back at the man and the mounting fury dissipates.

"I'm mad," he says in apology. "I'm mad all the time. But that's what you have to be in this world. Mankind is like dogs, not gods. As long as you don't get mad, they'll bite you. But stay mad, and you'll never get bitten. Dogs don't respect humility and sorrow."

"Beautifully said, but I'm still not letting you get in a bar fight."

He smiles and sways a little. "I'll have another whiskey."

I know it's not wise, but I'm also not about to cut off Jack Kerouac. "Sit tight," I say and return to the bar. Bob serves me, but looks over my shoulder with narrowed eyes. Jack is visibly drunk, swaying in his chair.

"This is his last," he says.

"Yes, thank you," I say. "I promise we'll be out of here soon."

When I return, Jack is once again trying to bore a hole into the back of a stranger at the bar, the same unsuspecting twenty-something from before.

"Jack!"

"What?"

"Do you want this drink?"

"Yes."

"Then you will not fight anyone. Do you hear me? You will not get into a fight today."

"I'm just protecting myself," he says with pleading eyes. If there is graffiti in the men's room that reads "Go home, Jack," it is likely merited.

"No, Jack. That man doesn't even know you're here. He's done nothing wrong. You will not fight him."

"Fine." He relents and I hand him the whiskey.

DRINKING WITH DEAD DRUNKS

"Here's to you," I say.

"Here's to me. Drunk and decadent and beyond all hope." Despite his words, he takes a sip with a smile.

"Hey, it wasn't all bad. You did a lot of good for a lot of people with your words. You must know that."

"I had nothing to offer anybody except my own confusion."

"Maybe they took some comfort in that."

"That still left me drunk and decadent and beyond all hope." His slur and sway grow stronger. "But you know what the thing is?"

"No, what's the thing?"

"The thing is, I was just living up to what they said I was."

"Maybe in part, but you certainly weren't a conformist."

"No, no. I was too Buddhist to be Catholic, too heathen to be Buddhist, too conservative to be a hippie, but too solitary to be a soldier. I didn't fit. I didn't fit with any of it."

"There's nothing wrong with standing behind what you believe."

"Of course not. I don't apologize for any of my beliefs. My fault, my failure, is not in the passions I had, but in my lack of control of them. It's not that I didn't try. Read *Big Sur*."

"You chronicled that in *Big Sur*, trying to control your passions."

"Yeah, but I was too far gone at that point, so it didn't work too well. I couldn't come back from it. Excuse me." He stands abruptly and I have a momentary fear that he's going to take a swing at the bar patron. Instead he makes his way to the restroom. I finish my beer and pay the tab. Jack returns but doesn't reclaim his seat, just stands precariously and finishes the last of his whiskey. "You'll never guess, but someone wrote a love letter to me in the bathroom."

"Yeah?" I play dumb. "What's it say?"

"It says, 'Go home, Jack.'" He sets his empty glass on the table and looks around the bar, thankfully without hostility, but his smile takes on a devilish hue. "But I'm already there."

Raymond Chandler
Gimlets and Gumshoes

BY ELAINE AMBROSE

I'm scheduled to sit at Raymond Chandler's table in the second floor bar of the Los Angeles Athletic Club but the stuffy guy at the reception desk is skeptical.

"Mr. Chandler's table requires a password."

Okay, I'm stumped. I didn't receive any secret word, so I improvise.

"Gimlet."

"Go right in, Miss. Take the stairs on the right." I feel a bit saucy because my guess was correct and I haven't been called Miss since 1982. I wink at the receptionist, but he's not impressed.

The second floor bar reeks of old aristocrats and older money. Black and white photographs of men who used to be important stretch across the dark, wood-paneled walls. Worn leather chairs circle marble-topped tables adorned with flickering candles where crystal ash trays once cradled imported cigars. Smoking is allowed only on the outside veranda, a decision that caused considerable heated debate and lost memberships. To placate the tobacco crowd, the Athletic Club sponsors quarterly cigar shows and arranges private trips to Cuba.

Raymond Chandler is sitting in the corner, an unlit pipe in his mouth. He motions me to come over and then calls to the bartender to bring two gimlets. I'm not surprised. He places the pipe on the table and shakes my hand.

"It's a pleasure to meet you," I say and sink into the soft chair. I wonder what a club membership costs.

"I'm not sure what you want to know," he says. "I just tell crime stories."

"But you do it so well!"

"So I've been told."

The bartender brings our gimlets in frosted old-fashioned glasses. We sip and nod our approval.

"I've always said that a real gimlet is half gin and half Rose's lime juice and nothing else. It beats martinis hollow," he says.

"Didn't your detective Philip Marlowe favor the gimlet in *The Long Goodbye*?"

"Correct. Marlowe loved them. And he preferred it with Rose's instead of fresh lime juice. It changed the way Americans now drink it."

We enjoy the cocktail's cool tartness. I could get used to sitting here.

"I'm curious about how you got into writing. Wasn't it after you were fired from a job as an oil company executive?"

"That's right. I got canned for drinking and being absent. It was during the Great Depression, so my timing wasn't the best. I wrote some short stories that were published in popular pulp magazines, and then in 1939 I wrote a novel titled *The Big Sleep*. That's when I introduced Philip Marlowe."

"Why did you decide to write the novel in first person?"

"I wanted to be Marlowe. It's that simple."

We grow comfortable with the atmosphere and conversation.

"The year after *The Big Sleep* you wrote *Farewell, My Lovely*. It was the basis for three motion pictures, and actor Dick Powell first starred as Marlowe. Didn't that lead to your screenwriting jobs?"

"Yes. I wrote *Double Indemnity* with Billy Wilder and the screenplay was nominated for an Academy Award. That's when I knew that writing was more fun than working for an oil company."

"I've heard about your request to get drunk to finish a screenplay."

"Paramount Studios was on my butt to finish the script for *The Blue Dahlia*. I couldn't create the ending and they were already in production. After years of being a crazy drunk, I was trying to stay sober but I told the producers I had writer's block and needed to get drunk. Paramount brought six secretaries to my house to wait on me. A doctor came to give me vitamin shots because I don't eat when I drink. They had limousines waiting outside to rush pages as soon as I finished them. We didn't have fax machines back then. I was totally wasted when I wrote the last page, and it's one of my best original scripts. It was nominated for an Academy Award."

"That's an interesting technique," I say. "Perhaps I'll try it sometime."

"Take your vitamins."

"Will do."

"The worst time I had working in Hollywood was with that fat bastard Alfred Hitchcock. I was writing the screenplay for *Strangers on a Train* and he threw my first two drafts into the trash while holding his nose. What an arrogant prick!"

"Is that why you left Los Angeles?"

"I moved to La Jolla in 1946 because it was serene and by the ocean and not next to L.A. That's where I wrote *The Long Goodbye*, my final Philip Marlowe novel."

"Do you want to talk about Cissy?"

Chandler gulps the last of his gimlet and orders two more. The bartender brings fresh glasses with a crystal bowl of pecans and cashews.

"I thought you might want a small snack."

I thank him and reach for the nuts, if only to keep me from grabbing the gimlet and swilling it in one gulp. I'm beginning to appreciate this cocktail. A lot.

"I met Cissy, her real name was Pearl Eugenie Pascal, in 1920.

DRINKING WITH DEAD DRUNKS

My mother disapproved because Cissy was married and eighteen years older. Those minor details didn't bother me. Cissy divorced her husband but my mother refused to sanction our marriage. We waited until my mother died and then we got married. My lovely Cissy died in 1954."

We raise a toast to Cissy and enjoy a long drink.

"You might think this is strange, but I couldn't bear to bury her remains. I was drunk for quite a while and eventually forgot about them. They stayed in a storage locker in the basement of Cypress View Mausoleum for several years."

"Yes, that is strange."

"I was so distraught that I attempted suicide in 1955. But I called the police first so they prevented my plan. That probably was a stupid act on my part."

"Attempting suicide or calling the police?"

"Either. Take your pick."

"Well, at least you had four more years to live."

"Yes, but I always loved Cissy. Even through all my affairs and dalliances. She was my true love."

"I've read that you died broke and didn't have enough money to be buried next to Cissy at Cypress View."

There is an awkward silence and I fear that the gimlet has attacked my good judgment. I start to apologize.

"It's okay," he says. "Just because a writer wins a few Academy Awards doesn't mean great riches will come. I was broke and so they buried me in Mount Hope Cemetery. But in 2011 Cissy's remains were moved over by some historians and Hollywood types. I think Aissa Wayne, John Wayne's daughter, was instrumental in getting us together under a shared gravestone. It doesn't really matter though, does it?"

The bartender appears just in time with our third cocktail. I scoop a handful of nuts and wash them down with the intoxicating gin and lime juice. I'm sleepy but determined to finish the interview on a positive note.

GIMLETS AND GUMSHOES

"I remember some of your famous lines. 'He had a heart as big as one of Mae West's hips.' Or, how about, 'The muzzle of the Luger looked like the mouth of the Second Street Tunnel.'"

"I love to write lyrical similes," he says. "For example, here's a line I wrote in *The King in Yellow*: I'm an occasional drinker, the kind of guy who goes out for a beer and wakes up in Singapore with a full beard."

"Joyce Carol Oates wrote that readers are captivated by your seductive prose."

"Maybe that's true, maybe not. I'm just a gumshoe out looking for clues in a crime story. If that's seductive, so be it."

As we finish our cocktails, he lifts his glass and holds it against the light. Then he recites a passage from *The High Window*:

"Then he picked the glass up and tasted it and sighed again and shook his head sideways with a half smile; the way a man does when you give him a drink and he needs it very badly and it is just right and the first swallow is like a peek into a cleaner, sunnier, bright world."

We pay the tab and leave the stuffiness of the Los Angeles Athletic Club. I notice that a mysterious fog is settling over the neighborhood and I watch as Chandler walks into the mist, fading into black and white. Like a pulp fiction detective, I begin to search for clues to solve the mystery of how the hell I'm going to get home.

DRINKING WITH DEAD DRUNKS

Truman Capote
We're Not in Kansas

BY AK TURNER

Truman Capote looks dead serious. His cheeks hang heavy under forceful eyes. He's close enough that I can study the lines creeping in horizons across his forehead. "I have a question," he says. His voice is high, light and quiet, a counterweight to the heft of his features. The contrast is frightening, like a little girl's doll with broken limbs and missing eyes.

"Y-yes," I stammer. This isn't what I expected. I'm trying not to be intimidated, questioning what I've gotten myself into. My eyes are wide; I hold my breath.

"Do I make you nervous?" he asks, then relents by stepping back a foot and indulging in a devilish and satisfied laugh. He smiles and his features no longer look heavy.

"Don't do that!" I whine.

Now he's the jovial little man I'd anticipated. A mischievous smile is his resting expression. His hair is combed neatly, a black bow tie with white polka dots punctuates the top of his crisp white shirt. He's tidy.

"You're short for a literary giant," I comment.

"I'm as tall as a shotgun and just as noisy."

"I guess I'm in for a treat, then."

"Yes, my dear, you are," he says as we take seats at the bar. "But

DRINKING WITH DEAD DRUNKS

I thought you said we were going to Studio 54. I was very much looking forward to that."

"I know, but Studio 54 doesn't really exist anymore. This is the closest thing to it." We're at a small bar upstairs from the original Studio 54, aptly named Upstairs at Studio 54. "And we're lucky they're even open. The original Studio 54 is now the Roundabout Theatre Company and this bar is closed when they have shows running. We landed at the right time."

"Hmm," he says, and the murmur is loaded with discontent.

"You wanted more of a party?" I ask.

"No, this is fine. I've had enough of parties, anyway."

"Sorry, it's no Black and White Ball. Besides, I don't know any celebrities."

"Now *that* was a party."

"You pissed off a few people with that one, didn't you?" I ask.

"Sure, but that's fine. It was my great, big, all-time spectacular present to me." Capote's eyes grow wide with excitement. "I held it at the Plaza Hotel, though really, where else would I have had it? It was the only decent ballroom left, don't you think so?"

"You know, I'm not really a New Yorker…" I say.

"I grew up in Monroeville, Alabama, but I know a decent ballroom when I see one. Anyway, the guest list was divine. It was exactly as I wanted it to be."

"Do you want a drink?" I ask.

"Of course I want a drink; I'm an alcoholic."

"I'll have a Guinness," I tell the bartender.

"And I'd like Justerini and Brooks whisky, neat."

"I'm sorry, what was that?" the bartender asks.

"Justerini and Brooks. Do you not have Justerini and Brooks? We may have to go somewhere else."

"One more time?" asks the bartender.

"Justerini and Brooks," says Capote.

"I've never heard of it, either," I say.

"Oh, fine, you're no fun. It's J&B whisky. I was just having a little fun."

"We have J&B," says the bartender.

"Of course you do," says Capote. "I'll have a J&B, neat."

Our drinks come quick, a combination of a sparse crowd and the bartender's desire to be done with us. I drink Guinness frighteningly fast, so as the bartender drops off the drinks, I put in the order for another round.

"Tell me about *Breakfast at Tiffany's*," I say.

"I'd done a great deal of experimental journalism, and *Tiffany's* was the beginning of moving past that and evolving into different forms of writing. I just always wanted to *evolve* in my writing. I enjoyed the writing itself. Of course, *finishing* a book is like taking a child into the backyard and shooting it."

"Who was Holly Golightly modeled after?"

"Oh, about half the women I knew in my life, but don't tell them that. There was a bit of my mother in there, too."

"What did you think of the movie?"

"I never saw Audrey in that role. It should have been Marilyn. That was always a part for Marilyn."

"Monroe?"

"Is there another Marilyn to whom I could possibly be referring?"

"Wait, so even after you saw the movie, you still didn't think that Audrey Hepburn should have played Holly Golightly?" I finish my Guinness and reach for the second.

"Marilyn," he states, and I understand that we've reached the end of the Holly Golightly discussion.

"Okay, so tell me about *In Cold Blood*. You know, for a minute I thought we should meet in Holcomb."

For a high-pitched man with a lisp, he has a surprisingly hearty laugh, which he lets loose at the mention of meeting in Kansas.

"You know, I arrived not too long after the murders. Really, they'd just happened. And it was nearly a disaster trying to get those people to talk to me. Thank God for Nelle. We took the train out there."

"I thought I read somewhere that Harper Lee went with you? That she helped you research *In Cold Blood*?"

"She did," he says with mild impatience. "Harper Lee's name was Nelle. If she'd published as Nelle Lee, she'd have been misidentified as Nellie. In any case, we were childhood friends back in Monroeville, and she was so endearing, she could get us into the homes of the people I needed to talk to. I might have success with that sort of thing in New York, but not in Kansas."

I sense Truman's excitement in his inability to hold still. He sways now as he speaks, both from side to side and front to back, eventually settling into a large, circular wobble.

"I got this idea of doing a really serious big work. It would be precisely like a novel, with a single difference: Every word of it would be true from beginning to end. This was my continuing attempt to evolve the writing form. In terms of a non-fiction novel, it was remarkable, I can look at it as an outsider and see that."

"Do you still think about the family that was killed?" I ask.

"Who? The Clutters? Of course. Just as I think about Dick Hickock and Perry Smith."

"The murderers?"

"Sure, there were only four shotgun blasts, but the end of six human lives."

My brow furrows at this.

"Remember," he continues, "I knew Hickock and Smith when they were alive. And I watched them hang. It can take an hour to die by hanging. It's not quick like you might think. Of course I think of them."

"There have been a lot of rumors about your relationship with Perry Smith," I say.

"Rumors are delicious."

We order a third round.

"You told me earlier that you are an alcoholic. What else are you?" I ask.

WE'RE NOT IN KANSAS

"Oh yes, I'm completely honest about who I am. I'm an alcoholic, a drug addict, a homosexual, and a genius." Our drinks arrive. "But I am not a saint."

"Cheers to that," I say. "So, it was after *In Cold Blood* that you threw your big Black and White Ball?"

"Yes, and I deserved it. That book nearly killed me. And even halfway through the book, I didn't know if it would amount to anything."

"Did you feel you were done then?" I ask, emboldened by alcohol.

Truman's face takes on the heavy look of our first meeting. "Of course not, I still wanted to evolve my writing. And I was doing it, too."

"With *Answered Prayers*?"

"Yes, with *Answered Prayers*."

"Because some say that all that celebrity killed your literary talent."

"That's jealousy. And completely backward. If anything, my literary talent killed my celebrity."

"How do you mean? I thought *In Cold Blood* made you a celebrity."

"It did, but *Answered Prayers* took it away."

"Well, when you write about people, about things they don't want you to write about, you're bound to raise their hackles."

"You can't get mad at a writer for what his characters say. Besides, all literature is gossip."

"Especially if those people are famous, elite, royalty type people."

"Well, I'm a writer. How could they think I wasn't going to write about them?"

"I don't know," I concede. "I wasn't there and I certainly didn't and don't know any of the famous people you rubbed elbows with. I think if you do write about them, in a less than flattering light, you're supposed to wait until they're dead."

DRINKING WITH DEAD DRUNKS

"I guess *you'd* know all about that," he says.

"Yeah," I offer a grin.

"That's all right," says Truman. He seems to be wobbling in an ever-expanding arc. "You can rub elbows with me."

"Thanks." I smile and we physically rub our elbows together, a sure sign that it's time to order another round. "So, with *Answered Prayers*, I know you published a few chapters of it in *Esquire* before you died. Was it near completion?"

"Yes," he says. "It was near completion for *years*."

"Most writers can identify with that."

"And it's a good thing I did publish those chapters in *Esquire*. There was no way I could wait until my subjects were dead. I beat them all to the grave."

"I guess you have a point there."

"I can only imagine what that prick Vidal said after I died."

"Nothing comes to mind," I lie, well aware that Gore Vidal described Capote's death as a good career move. We finish the drinks in front of us. I'm not sure if it's a third, fourth or fifth round.

"Life is a moderately good play with a badly written third act," says Capote. "Maybe I left the show before it turned really ugly."

John Cheever
Letting It Breathe

BY ELAINE AMBROSE

John Cheever wants to meet at Trattoria Toscana in Boston for three reasons: He once taught at Boston University, he once lived in Italy and loves Italian food, and (perhaps the biggest reason) the bar only serves wine and beer. His former habit of drinking a bottle of scotch every day was literally killing him, so he's trying to cut back to just wine and beer. A devout wino, I eagerly comply.

We find a table in the corner and order a bottle of Amarone from the Masi Vineyard near the Tuscany region of Italy. The waiter brings the wine in a decanter and advises us to let it breathe for at least twenty minutes to release the maximum essence and robust taste. I call bullshit after ten minutes and pour two glasses. We smell, we swirl, we sip. The wine is exquisite.

"Excellent choice," he says after savoring the first drink of the bold, luscious wine.

"This is my favorite," I reply. "I usually save it for special occasions and I think that would include an interview with a famous dead writer."

He chuckles and takes another sip.

"You're a bit of an enigma. Your stories are very critical of the American middle class, yet that's the life you came from and the life you lived with your family."

DRINKING WITH DEAD DRUNKS

"I have been a storyteller since the beginning of my life, rearranging facts in order to make them more significant. I have improvised a background for myself – genteel, traditional – and it is generally accepted."

"So you invented yourself as an author?"

"You could say that I resemble my characters. I know how to look behind the pleasing façade of proper people and uncover their weaknesses and debauchery. I identify with the average man who is tormented with insecurity and ambiguity."

"I've read that your father lost everything in the Great Depression and that your mother needed to work to support the family. You never forgot the humiliation."

"True. It was painful to watch my father lose his dignity and my parents eventually separated. I purposely flunked out of prep school in Massachusetts but that experience resulted in my first published work – a short story titled 'Expelled.' It was published in 1930 in *The New Republic*."

"So maybe trauma can be a good thing?"

"Yes. The magazine's editor arranged for me to attend Yaddo, a writers' colony in Saratoga. From there I developed a relationship with *The New Yorker* and the magazine published 119 of my stories."

We empty the bottle into our wine glasses, and I motion for the waiter to bring us another Amarone. The smooth wine helps me wade through the complex conversation, and I want to get the serious stuff out of the way before I get too silly.

"Tell me about Cheever Country."

"Writers have the unique opportunity to create their own worlds," he says. "My characters live in the world of Cheever Country where I control their thoughts and actions. I take regular people in typical situations and wait for calamity. It's a bit of a rush, actually."

"I've read that you had a unique writing routine when you were getting established."

"Yes," he says and then takes a long drink. "Every day for five

LETTING IT BREATHE

years I would dress in my only suit and take the elevator down to my apartment building's basement. There I worked in the maid's room while she was gone tending to her duties around the building. I stripped to my underwear and wrote until lunchtime. Then I would get dressed and go back to my room. That was the disciplined routine I needed to focus on writing. It worked because the stories I finished down in the basement in my boxer shorts helped me receive an advance from Random House to finish a novel."

A full decanter arrives at our table and we wait only five minutes for it to breathe. Patience is not a virtue among famous or aspiring writers.

"I love Italian wine," he says after a slow swallow. "I lived in Italy in 1957. I took my wife and baby daughter there using the proceeds from selling the movie rights to 'The Housebreaker of Shady Hill.' Who knew a housebreaker would have the power to send me to Italy?"

"Sounds like one of your ironic short stories."

"Yes, it does. But life got crazy after we returned to the states. My wife and I weren't getting along. She claimed I was a neurotic, narcissistic, egocentric, and friendless man. She said I was so deeply involved in my own defensive illusions that I caused her to be a manic-depressive wife. What kind of crap is that?"

"Sounds like you needed counseling."

"We went to counseling but the counselor agreed with her! That's why I stopped going to therapy and started drinking a bottle of scotch every day. Being bi-sexual may have added to our troubles."

"That could have a negative impact on a marriage," I agree.

We sip our wine and I contemplate the next line of questioning. I decide not to ask about his suicidal days while he was a professor at Boston University or his admission to Smithers Alcoholic Rehabilitation Unit in New York or about his massive heart attack or about the cancer. I have no intention of witnessing what his wife referred to as his neurotic, narcissistic side. Especially not while enjoying a fine wine.

"How did you like appearing on the cover of *Newsweek*?" I ask, desperate for a positive reaction.

"That was in 1977," he beams. "My novel *Falconer* was number one on the *New York Times* best-seller list for three weeks!"

We clink glasses in mutual celebration. The wine is getting better with every sip.

"Of course the plot of *Falcone*r wasn't pretty. It describes a writing instructor recovering from alcoholism and drug addiction, and the book contains rough language, violence, and references to homosexuality in a prison setting. It's not children's literature."

"Definitely not," I respond, wondering where I could find the novel.

I decide to acknowledge another accolade. "In 1978, you won a Pulitzer Prize for your short story collection. Did that finally convince you that your writing had merit?"

"I owe my life to literature," he says, becoming philosophical. "Literature has been the salvation of the damned, literature has inspired and guided lovers, routed despair and can perhaps in this case save the world."

We raise our glasses in a solemn salute to literature. It goes down easy.

"For me, a page of good prose is where one hears the rain and the noise of battle. It has the power to give grief or universality that lends it a youthful beauty."

Another toast. Another sip. The decanter is empty and there is nothing more to discuss.

"Thank you, John Cheever," I say as I call for the check. "It's been nice chatting with you."

"You're more than welcome," he responds. "And thanks for not asking about those depressing incidents at Boston University."

"No problem."

"And thanks for not talking about that miserable time in rehab."

"Wouldn't think of it."

LETTING IT BREATHE

"Finally, I do appreciate you not wondering about the bi-sexuality, the massive heart attack, or painful death from cancer."

"I think you just covered all that."

"Well then, thanks for nothing."

We shake hands and part ways. I holler "Ciao" as I overhear him ask the bartender where he can get a good bottle of scotch.

DRINKING WITH DEAD DRUNKS

JAMES JOYCE
DOGS AND THUNDER

BY AK TURNER

"Where are we going?" James Joyce asks. His voice is soft and I find myself inching closer to hear him. Our sleeves brush cordially past one another.

"To Shakespeare and Company," I answer.

"Really?"

"Well, it's not the original one," I amend. "But it was named Shakespeare and Company as a tribute to the one you knew."

We walk along the Seine and then stop in front of the shop. I can see the Cathedral of Notre Dame from where I stand.

"Yes," he says. "This is not the same store." His voice is neutral; he's not saddened by the current Shakespeare and Company.

The bookstore feels like a place of comfort for lovers of words. We enter and are drawn to study the spines lining shelves all around us. It smells as a bookstore should.

A blonde woman is speaking to a disheveled young man. She has a beautiful face, perfect mouth, made all the more radiant by the scores of books threatening to swallow us. Her eyes have energy in them, while the man looks tired. They seem to be discussing a short story, one that she read long ago, but that he just discovered. He tells her he's leaving for a bit, but that he'll return for a later shift. I make my way toward the stairs. I'm on the fourth step, Joyce behind me on the first, when we hear the young man call, "Thanks, Sylvia," as he exits.

"Sylvia!" Joyce whispers.

I look back at him, still making my way up the stairs. "Yes, but not the same Sylvia."

"Of course not," he smiles, "it couldn't be."

We reach the second floor and another world of words. A pair of chairs waits quietly in seclusion and we sit.

"Sylvia – the first Sylvia, not the one down there – published *Ulysses* for me. It was banned elsewhere."

"But not in Ireland." I take a bottle of white wine, still moderately chilled, from my backpack. Normally I'd be embarrassed by a screw top versus a cork, but Joyce seems intrigued by it. I pour the wine into plastic cups. Shakespeare and Company isn't the place you go for a drink, but I have a hunch we won't be bothered.

"No," says Joyce, sipping the wine. "It wasn't banned in Ireland, just the United States and the United Kingdom."

"Don't worry, it's everywhere now," I say.

"I have suspicions that those who banned it did not read it first," he says.

"You're probably right," I agree. "I think they objected to that one part about masturbation."

"Yes, *The Little Review* ran it. And a particular group was riled by it. The New York Society for the Suppression of Vice. Are they still calling literature obscene?"

"They're long gone."

"I'll drink to that," he says. After a moment his brow furrows. "Some people called the book pornography."

"And others called it a masterpiece."

"And others called it incomprehensible," he adds.

"They're just a bunch of dolts," I say, not adding that would make me a bit of a dolt myself.

"Let's drink to dolts," he says. And we do.

"Still," I say, "it was never banned in Ireland."

DOGS AND THUNDER

He studies me with narrowed eyes for a moment. "You wanted us to meet in Dublin, didn't you?"

"Well, I can't help it! You wrote *Dubliners*; so *yes*, I wanted to meet in Dublin."

"I didn't set foot in Dublin for the last twenty-nine years of my life; I'm not about to do so now."

"Okay," I relent.

"And I think this," he gestures to the bookshop, "is entirely appropriate."

"I promise I won't ask you to set foot in a church, either."

"Ha!" he laughs. "We'll have to drink to that, as well."

I like James Joyce, both as a writer and a man. His work alternately depresses and confuses me, but that doesn't necessarily turn me away from it. As a man, I find him calm and kind, despite a thread of stress that seems to run just below his skin. The trouble, I guess, stems from the idea of banned books.

"Do you study everyone like this?" he asks.

"Oh, sorry," I say, realizing that I've been staring at him intently. He has a long face, gray at the temples, and little round glasses that seem to hold his eyes in his head. The picture of this man is wholly appropriate for a writer.

"I'm not troubled by it," he says. "But we appear to be lacking in wine."

"That is troubling," I say, "but only for a moment." I bring a second bottle of white from my bag. This one has lost all pretense of being chilled, but after the first bottle, we don't really care.

"May I?" asks Joyce.

"Of course," I hand him the bottle. He unscrews the cap and I again silently chastise myself for not buying something fancier. The wine isn't in a box, though, so that's something.

I want to ask him about *Finnegans Wake*, but fear that will reveal the full extent of my stupidity. He reads my mind and saves me the ask.

"*Finnegans Wake* took me seventeen years to write."

"Ouch," I say.

"They were difficult years, made worse by my failing eyesight."

"Double ouch."

"I did finish it in time," he mutters, referring to his death two years after its publication.

"There's still a lot of discussion over that one."

"More of the masterpiece versus incomprehensible debate, I'd guess."

"Well, yes," I admit. "Some people argue over whether or not you had distinguishable characters and whether or not the book was all a dream. And if so, was it all the dream of one character, if you even had characters?"

"What do you think?" he asks, and this is my great fear.

I cop out by way of wine. "I think even debating it makes my head hurt."

"The critics were also troubled by my use of language, but you can't describe the night, and what happens to our souls when we are unconscious, in regular language. That wouldn't be a true depiction of night and dream."

"I think people will always object when writers play with language."

"It's not as if I'm redefining English. Read the book, then have your language back. I'm not destroying it for good, just for the sake of a night."

A dog barks on the street outside. Joyce tenses. I know that this is one of two great fears. I top off both of our cups and he smiles in thanks.

We finish the second bottle and I find myself straining to keep my eyes open. Joyce notices this.

"Shall we explore this store for a moment?" he suggests.

"Yes," I agree. Standing revives me. We peruse the shelves, but I struggle to focus on the titles. The spines seem so tiny, and reading sideways is a challenge.

We round a corner and find a bed, right there in the bookshop.

DOGS AND THUNDER

Well, not necessarily a bed, but a cot.

"Is this here for... us?" he asks. "Did they know you'd need a rest?"

"No, but I know why it's here. This is for the Tumbleweeds."

"The Tumbleweeds?"

"Yes. Sylvia – the current Sylvia, not the one you knew – she allows aspiring writers to stay here. They get a place to sleep in exchange for helping out a bit with the shop."

"That's marvelous," he says.

"And they have to read and write every day," I add, "that's one of the conditions."

"Maybe you should pretend you're a Tumbleweed for a few minutes," he says.

"Damn, I'm sorry," I say. "This wine just hit me hard."

"No need for apologies. Just rest a bit."

I collapse on the cot and wonder if this is the bed of the young man we saw speaking with Sylvia when we entered. I wonder what he or Sylvia will do if they find me. I'm too intoxicated to care. I curl up in the fetal position and Joyce pats me on the shoulder.

"Rest a while and you'll be fine."

"I'll sleep like *The Dead* for sure."

I hear a low rumble and recognize it as distant thunder. And this, I know, is his second great fear. I open my eyes but remain in the fetal position.

"Are you going to be okay?" I ask.

"We're screwed," he says. "I'm sure we're screwed."

I worry for a moment that he's going to panic and fall apart completely, that *he'll* need the cot for the fetal position, but then recognize this as a line from *The Dead* and smile.

"You're going to be okay," I state.

"Yes, but I do have to leave now. In light of the coming storm, I have to leave *right* now."

"I understand," I close my eyes again. "I'm just going to rest here for a little bit."

He pats my shoulder once again. "*Beannacht libh*, blessings to you," he says, and takes his leave.

WILLIAM FAULKNER
AS I LAY DYING AFTER FOUR MINT JULEPS

BY ELAINE AMBROSE

It's my first visit to Oxford, Mississippi, so I tackle the tourist to-do list. First, I see William Faulkner's grave in St. Peter's Cemetery and leave an empty whiskey bottle and scatter some pennies. Then, I drive to the University of Mississippi and purchase a set of "Ole Miss" wine glasses. Finally, I stop at the City Grocery Restaurant in the Courthouse Square for some shrimp and grits before meeting William Faulkner upstairs in the City Grocery Bar.

He arrives on time and we find a table underneath a lazy fan. I'm not used to the humidity so I remove my jacket and blot my face with a napkin. He remains unfazed in his suit, starched shirt and tie. An ebullient waiter hustles over with glasses and a pitcher of iced water and lemon slices. I pour and swallow a glass of water before Faulkner can order drinks.

"I suggest some mint juleps," he says with a slight Southern drawl. "They're quite refreshing and sure to subdue this heat." The waiter scurries off while I gulp more water.

"Mint juleps sound wonderful!" I attempt to act nonchalant before I melt into a greasy puddle on the floor. The waiter returns with two tall frosted glasses, and the mixture of mint, sweet syrup and bourbon over ice quells the jungle heat of Mississippi. I can tell we'll need another round, soon.

"Welcome to Oxford," Faulkner says as he gently stirs his drink. He smiles when he notices my julep is almost gone. "I'm happy you like our Southern drink."

"It's a pleasure to be here," I answer truthfully. "And this mint julep is fantastic!"

"I'm used to the climate. I was born in Mississippi and spent most of my life here. Did you know that I'm named after my great-granddaddy who was a Confederate Colonel in the Civil War? And that I was raised by a wonderful black woman named Caroline Barr?"

"No," I respond between sips. "I was raised in Idaho and things are a bit different over there."

"Of course. We're all products of our own heritage. That's why I created a fictional place called Yoknapatawpha County modeled after my childhood home, and most of my short stories and novels take place there."

I slurp the last of my drink and smile as the waiter brings us a second round. I'm finally cool enough to stop rolling the water jug across my forehead.

"One of your best known novels is *The Sound and the Fury*. Why that title?"

"It's taken from a line in Shakespeare's great play *Macbeth*. I used a similar technique for *As I Lay Dying*. That phrase comes from a poem in Homer's *Odyssey*."

"Did you really write *As I Lay Dying* in six weeks?"

"Yes. I wanted to experiment with stream of consciousness. The book is narrated by fifteen different characters, including a dead one in a casket. At the time, it seemed like a creative gimmick to make money."

"Very bold of you."

"Well, yes, but I enjoy creating various narrative styles. *The Sound and the Fury* uses four styles, including the voices of three people and one third person omniscient point of view. This method makes it difficult to keep track of the plot so I make meticulous

AS I LAY DYING AFTER FOUR MINT JULEPS

charts and notes for each chapter. I've even written story panels on the walls of my study to keep track of what is happening."

"That seems so complicated," I say. "But that's why you're regarded as one of the best American writers and why you won the Nobel Prize in Literature and two Pulitzer Prizes for fiction."

Faulkner finishes his first drink and starts on the second. I'm still ahead of him and signal for a third round. I convince myself that it's healthy because of all the fresh mint.

"Awards don't mean anything to me," he says. "In fact, I didn't tell my own daughter about the Nobel Prize. She learned about it at school. I donated part of the prize money to establish a fund to support and encourage new fiction writers."

"That fund now is called the PEN/Faulkner Award for Fiction," I say, proud to remember some of my research after two strong mint juleps.

"I also established a scholarship fund to help educate African-American teachers at Rust College," he says. "That was to honor Caroline Barr, the good woman who helped raise me. I include her wisdom and character in many of my novels."

Faulkner has picked up the pace and we're even on the third drink. I think bourbon is a fantastic invention.

"Why the name change?" I suddenly remember an interesting tidbit from my research.

"My last name was spelled without the 'u' so I changed it to the English version as a ploy to get into the Royal Air Force," he says. "But being only 5'5" worked against me. And World War I ended by the time I was ready so I never served. Besides, it seemed as if typesetters often misspelled my name so I left it as Faulkner."

"Yes, I like it that way," I agree. "You were a prolific writer of novels and short stories. What was behind your drive to write?"

"Truthfully, I needed the money. My magazine articles paid regularly so I wrote and submitted as many as I could while also working on novels. I think I finished twenty novels and a dozen collections of short stories. I also wrote plays, essays, drama, and poetry.

Say, where is that waiter?"

"I think bourbon is a fantastic invention," I say, trying to remember if I've said it before. The waiter brings our fourth drink and we are lavish with our appreciation.

Faulkner finally loosens his tie and unbuttons his starched collar.

"Careful," I warn. "Soon you'll be removing that jacket!"

He laughs, takes off the jacket, and rolls up his shirt sleeves.

"Did you know I received a 'D' in English as a student at Ole Miss?" He laughs.

"Obviously that didn't hurt your writing career."

"I didn't like college. I flunked out but my father got me back into school. I missed most of my classes, but don't write about that."

"Okay," I say, savoring the wonderful invention of bourbon.

"And don't write about my extra-marital affairs. Or my alcoholism."

"Do you drink?" I ask in a lame attempt to be funny.

"I usually got drunk after every writing project was completed," he says. "Maybe that's why I wrote so much. I had a bit of a drinking problem."

We laugh and finish our mint juleps. I am about to say something when he interrupts.

"Isn't bourbon a wonderful invention?" he asks. I nod and faintly remember hearing that somewhere before.

"Any last tidbits of advice before I stumble to my room?" I ask.

"Yes. Read, read, read. Read everything – trash, classics, good and bad, and see how they do it. Just like a carpenter who works as an apprentice and studies the master. Read! You'll absorb it. Then write. If it's good, you'll find out. If it's not, throw it out of the window."

I pay the bill and we stand to leave. I'm grateful that my room is within easy walking distance.

"One more thing," he says. "Don't be a writer. Be writing. Oh, wait. Another thing: If a story is in you, it has to come out."

I thank him again and turn to leave.

AS I LAY DYING AFTER FOUR MINT JULEPS

"Just one more," he calls after me. "A writer needs three things, experience, observation, and imagination, any two of which, at times any one of which, can supply the lack of the others."

I quickly scribble his quotes in my notebook. I hope the comments are legible.

"Now I'm done," he says and slings his jacket over his shoulder. "Unless you want to add a fourth thing a writer needs."

"Mint juleps," we declare in unison. He pats me on the back and walks out the door. I grin because I am in tune with William Faulkner and with the universe and my bed is nearby underneath a humming fan.

DRINKING WITH DEAD DRUNKS

FREDERICK EXLEY
THAT LONG MALAISE

"Why the hell are we in Watertown?" he asks. The New York sky is heavy, thick with an oppressive gray. "We should be at the Lion's Head in Greenwich Village."

"I hate to tell you, but the Lion's Head closed."

"No!" He stops as if socked in the gut.

"I thought maybe you'd want to come to your hometown."

"Ugh." His shoulders slump.

"But this is your home," I protest.

"Home is a flimsy thing."

"I'm sorry. It'll be okay. Come on, let's get a drink."

We enter a bar called Mick's Place on Factory Street. It's dim as a bar should be. And something doesn't smell quite right. We claim two stools and the bartender approaches. He's young, but haggard with heavy lids that speak of heavy drinking.

"What would you like?" He throws a pair of coasters in front of us.

"Double vodka on the rocks with a splash of tonic," says Fred.

"I'll have a vodka and soda," I say. "With a lime, please?"

"Sure," says the bartender.

Left to one another, Exley turns away from me and looks up at a television. Cars buzz monotonously around a track.

DRINKING WITH DEAD DRUNKS

"Let me guess," I venture. "You were hoping for football?"

A smile emerges from within his grizzled beard. "I am a fan."

"I have more bad news for you. Frank Gifford had a bit of a fall from grace."

"What are you talking about?" he asks. "Frank retired long ago."

"It was more of a tabloid story," I explain. "He got caught in an affair."

"You can't trust the tabloids. I'm sure they made up whatever the story was, just to sell a few papers."

"Well, it was a little more than that. They had video footage and audio recordings."

He straightens up on his bar stool, his stocky frame growing an inch in Gifford's defense. "So, he steps out once. Not the end of the world."

"It was a week-long, hotel room affair with a stewardess." I don't know why I'm compelled to push this issue, but I can't help myself. And I haven't yet had a drink.

"What have you got against Frank Gifford?" Exley demands. "He's a Hall of Famer! Twelve seasons with the Giants. Eight Pro Bowls and five NFL Championship games. Give the guy a break!"

The bartender returns with eyes so bloodshot they give me a headache, but the drinks are welcome.

"Please bring me another," Exley says, before taking a sip. The bartender nods as if this is not an uncommon request. I make a mental note never to return to this bar.

"Cheers," I say as a peace offering and kiss my glass to his.

"So, which are you?" he asks. "Are you an Exley or a Gifford?"

"Excuse me?"

"Are you a suffering poet or a cheerful drone?"

"Gosh." I sip my drink, wishing I'd asked for vodka other than well. "Are those my only choices?"

"Yes. Don't try and concoct any others because they don't exist."

"I can't be a cheerful poet?"

THAT LONG MALAISE

"No," laughs Exley. "That's cheating."

"I guess I'm a little of both, depending on when you catch me." He eyes me with suspicion. "Again, cheating."

"So what does it mean to be Fred Exley?" I ask.

He thinks for a moment, nods at the bartender as his second drink arrives. "It means you're doomed to be a spectator in life as well as sports." He smirks under sad brown eyes.

"That's not true," I say. "You weren't just a spectator. You wrote *A Fan's Notes*. You had *success*."

"Success!" He laughs heartily at this, so much so that he's compelled to wipe at the corners of his eyes. When he catches his breath, he grows suddenly serious. "*A Fan's Notes* was important. Everyone should read my book. But it was the damn publishers, they didn't do adequate publicity."

"You had fun, though. You had recognition."

"I had fun drinking in New York, but I'm still pissed at the publishers. That's why the other two didn't do well, because of the publishers. *Pages from a Cold Island*, that was their fault."

While few might agree with him, I know that most literary criticism claims his genius was enough for only one book. After *A Fan's Notes*, the others paled. I'm not voicing this, though. It would be cruel. He's fragile as it is, and I'm feeling guilty for telling him about Gifford's demise in the public eye. At least, in the female public eye.

He signals the bartender for another round, then points to me and says, "And she'll have a double this time."

"I will?"

"Yes," says Fred, "you will."

"Despite your overall depression, I bet you can be charming when you want to be."

"Of course I can. But I don't drink for wit, I drink because I'm agitated. *You* agitate me."

"Sorry."

"Alcohol is a depressant, it brings me down from sobriety."

DRINKING WITH DEAD DRUNKS

The bartender delivers the next round, Exley's third and my second. I wish I would have spoken up and asked for a more expensive vodka, especially in light of Exley's assertion that I'll have a double, but I don't want to seem prissy. As the bartender turns away, I see a trail of blood begin to snake down from his nose.

"Oh, uh, excuse me," I say. He doesn't hear me. "I think you have a bit of a…"

"Hey," Fred barks. "Your fucking nose is bleeding!"

"Thanks," I whisper.

"Thanks!" the bartender barks back, then retreats to the bathroom to clean up. I make a second mental note to never ever return to this bar, just in case the first mental note becomes lost somehow. With the bartender gone, Exley stands up from his barstool and walks behind the bar.

"What are you doing?" I ask.

"Settle yourself," he says.

"You're not going to do anything *illegal*, are you?" He's dead, so I can't see any reason for him to rob the place, but that's where my mind is headed.

"Again, settle yourself."

He grabs something and comes back from behind the bar, plants his stocky frame on his stool. In his hand is the remote, and he aims it at the television, ready to rid us of Nascar. He flips through the channels, past an infomercial for the Total Gym and a shopping channel selling the ugliest jewelry I've ever seen.

"There must be some football on, somewhere," he says.

"I hope not," I admit. "I really have no interest in watching football with you."

He looks at me then. "Well, *that's* depressing."

"Just being honest."

"Oh!" I'm afraid he's found football, but that's not it at all. I look up to see Diane Sawyer on the television. "I once spent the night with Diane Sawyer," he says.

"You did?"

"Yes."

"I don't believe you."

"Okay, I didn't, but it made for a great essay."

"Oh yeah, I know what you're talking about. The one in *Esquire*."

"In all seriousness though, I bet if I bit into Diane Sawyer, she would bleed pure butterscotch."

"Can I write that?" I ask.

"Go get your own line."

"*Really* in all seriousness, tell me about the women in your life."

"What's to tell? I had my share of girls, spent years drowning in a pastel nightmare of them."

"I'm definitely writing that."

"She's still perfect," he says, gazing up at Sawyer.

The bartender returns, but looks like a child left to clean himself. The bloody nose has ceased, but a crimson crust surrounds one nostril. I almost hate him for it.

"We would like two more," says Fred.

"But I would like mine with Absolut this time," I add.

Exley looks sidelong at me with a smirk, but withholds any words of judgment.

The bartender nods and is about to make our drinks when he notices the remote on the bar and replacement of Nascar with Diane Sawyer. I brace myself for a reprimand, but the bloody bartender looks as taken with Sawyer as Exley. He's spellbound for a moment, then returns to duty.

Exley doesn't speak again until Diane Sawyer disappears. He does drink, though, and the drinks keep coming. I lose track of how much we've consumed. My head is light and has a tingle buried inside. I check to see if my purse is still hanging on the back of my chair. It is, of course, but I'm drunk and feeling vulnerable. The television is duplicated now, two images of it. One where the television screen should be, then a second off to the right and a little bit higher. I try to close one eye to bring it back into focus, but then relent. In double vision I watch an ornery judge preside over trashy disputes.

"Ugh," I say. "This is so fitting for this bar."

In response, Exley picks up the remote and turns off the television.

"Thanks for that," I add.

"You know, I couldn't help but wonder on some level if today was going to result in men in white coats coming to take me away."

"I'm not that crafty," I slur. "And believe me, I have no place in doing any kind of intervention on anyone else."

"Actually, I didn't much mind the mental hospitals," he says. His speech is precise and I wish he'd show his drunkenness like mine.

"You didn't *mind* the mental hospitals?" This is not what I expect.

"Not at all," he asserts. "I could easily have spent my life there. It's not so bad."

"What makes a mental hospital so great?" I ask.

"You're cared for and you have a captive audience. Not a bad situation for a struggling writer, much better than dealing with the damn publishers."

"Huh." I ponder this, but my mind is sodden.

"You're drunk," he says.

"Yes, Fred. I am drunk." I take another drink. "I wish you would be, too. It's awfully lonely."

"Don't worry," he says, "I'm on my way."

"Good."

"You seem past the point of any good debate, though."

"I'm sorry, but yes. What are we supposed to debate, anyhow?"

"I don't know," says Fred. "I was just waiting for you to give me a good verbal spanking."

"If I stand up, I'll fall down. And my mind is…"

"Mush?"

"I was going to say porridge. My mind is porridge, so I don't think any verbal spanking, or any spanking for that matter, is forthcoming. Sorry."

THAT LONG MALAISE

"That's all right," says Exley. "Maybe next time."

He signals the bartender for yet another round. In terms of drinking, Exley is a champion, a player. He's a Gifford. But it's also part of what relegated him to spectator in terms of the rest of the world. I'm so drunk that I know I won't be conscious long enough to see Exley at his worst, as a terrible drunk. It's probably better that way. I want to put an end to this long malaise of an afternoon. I like Fred, but it's time for me to go. The bartender calls me a cab. The cabbie helps me to the car.

"Bye, Fred," I say.

He smiles at me from within the depths of his beard, and his eyes look happy for a moment.

"Take care, Butterscotch."

DRINKING WITH DEAD DRUNKS

O. Henry
Satire and Cirrhosis

BY ELAINE AMBROSE

I walk into Pete's Tavern in New York and am appreciably delighted to find the quintessential watering hole for drinkers who write, and vice versa. The forty-foot wooden bar curves along one wall underneath a brass chandelier that is more than one hundred years old. Hammered tin squares cover the ceiling, and the walls are lined with faded photographs of famous and infamous patrons who have frequented the tavern since 1864.

O. Henry is waiting for me in a booth near the back of the main room, and I introduce myself and scoot across the wooden bench to sit down. I recognize him by the handlebar moustache from his stoic photographs. He's wearing a dark wool suit and a white shirt with a large starched collar. His hair is parted in the middle and shows early streaks of gray. There is a sardonic and hapless manner about him, and I wait for him to speak.

"I hope you don't mind but I've ordered us drinks," he says. "Have you ever had a Sazerac cocktail?"

I shake my head no and ask how it's made.

"I first had this cocktail in New Orleans," he says. "It's a concoction of rye whiskey, syrup made from sugar and water, and bitters with a twist of lemon. Oh, and never have it with ice."

Our drinks arrive and I sip slowly, not quite ready for whiskey and syrup. It's tart and sweet, similar to a whiskey sour. I can tell that O. Henry likes the cocktail as he drinks, closes his eyes, and smiles.

"Just the right combination of syrup and bitters," he mutters and opens his eyes. "Some bartenders use cognac but whiskey is the best liquor to use in this drink."

He is already half finished with the drink and waves at the bartender to start another round. Then he runs his fingers over the wooden tabletop, fingering each nick and stain as if stroking an old lover. We sip in silence for a moment as I decide that I really like the drink.

"In this very booth I wrote *The Gift of the Magi*," he says. "Sometimes I delight myself because I never know what the surprise ending will be until I write it."

"You are famous for wit and irony," I say. "Was *Magi* your favorite short story?"

"Oh, heavens no," he answers. "I published more than 600 stories – often writing a story a week for the *New York World Sunday Magazine*. I'll always be fond of my first collection of short stories titled *Cabbages and Kings*. Each one relates to the other stories to advance the plot of the book."

"Didn't you write *Cabbages and Kings* while you were running from the law?"

"Well, yes," he admits. "There was this unfortunate incident when I was fired from the First National Bank of Austin for embezzlement. But I was innocent. It was just sloppy bookkeeping on my part."

"So you left your wife and child and fled to Honduras?" I'm on my second drink and can tell that the whiskey is prompting a bold line of questions.

He shrugs his shoulders. "I didn't know what else to do. I stayed in a quaint hotel in Trujillo and wrote. But I returned when I learned that my wife was dying from tuberculosis."

"Noble decision."

SATIRE AND CIRRHOSIS

"In 1898 I was sentenced to five years in prison at the Ohio Penitentiary in Columbus. But it wasn't so bad because I had been a pharmacist and worked in the prison hospital, and I had my own room instead of a cell. I wrote and published fourteen stories while incarcerated so I could help support my young daughter."

"Is that why you changed your name from William Sydney Porter to O. Henry?"

"Yes. I used the pseudonym on a Christmas story that was published in *McClure's Magazine* in 1899. I didn't think a Christmas story would be well-received if written by a convicted felon."

"How did you arrive at O. Henry?"

"I wanted a dignified name, so I looked through the newspaper society pages and found the last name of Henry. I wanted a short first name and 'O' is about as short as you can get. Some publications list me as Oliver Henry, but it's really just 'O' with a period. After I was released from jail I kept the name because so many of my stories had been published as O. Henry."

"You've had your share of heartache," I say as we both finish our drinks. The bartender responds with another round.

"Yes, my mother and wife both died from tuberculosis, and my son died at birth. But my daughter Margaret Porter is doing fine. She was never told that I was in jail, just away on business."

"What did you do after you were released from prison in 1901?"

"I moved to New York City to be near my publishers, and I wrote more than 380 stories. I prefer to use ordinary people, including policemen and waitresses, as characters in my writing. New York is a great place to people-watch for fresh ideas. I loiter in hotel lobbies and observe how people interact."

"You also remarried your high school sweetheart."

"Yes, I found Sarah again in 1908. But she didn't like the fact that I was a drunk so she left me. Cirrhosis of the liver killed me in 1910. I still regret that."

"I would regret that, too," I say, easing back on the drink. I decide to end the interview with a happier theme.

"*The Ransom of Red Chief* is my favorite," I say. "Two men kidnap a ten-year-old boy who is so obnoxious that the kidnappers eventually pay the father to take back the kid. Genius!"

"Yes." Henry smiles. "As a young man desperate for work I once took a job as a babysitter. I gleaned a massive amount of material from that experience."

"Any last thoughts for today?" I ask while trying to focus on his face. The whiskey gives me double-vision and I blink rapidly to stay alert. He blinks back, equally disabled.

"Irony lives in my stories and in my life," he answers. "There are at least three schools named after me as well as the O. Henry Hall owned by the University of Texas. There is a feature film made of five of my stories, and the O. Henry Award is a prestigious annual prize awarded for the best written short story."

"What's so ironic about that?" I ask, personally delighted that my sodden brain and rubbery tongue can manage a three-syllable word.

He looks smug. "Not bad for a drunken convict."

Charles Bukowski
The Mickey Mouse Club

BY AK TURNER

I'm in love with The Library Bar, but Bukowski is not. I can tell this before I reach him. His disdain is perceptible from the front door. While I fall completely for the low lighting, comfort, books and leather, Bukowski senses fraud.

"Charles?" I ask as I approach, though of course it's him.

"It's Hank. No one calls me Charles. You should know that." He draws out select words, speaks in metered rhythm. He has a nice voice, soothing but dangerous.

"Right, then, Hank."

"We should have met at a dive bar. Couldn't you find a dive bar in L.A.? I'm sure they're still around."

"Do you want to leave?" I ask.

"No, I'm not leaving. Sit down. I already ordered a few bottles. We're having three bottles of their cheapest red; that's for starters. I'm sure you drink red wine. Do you drink red wine?"

"Yes."

"Good. I like the really cheap shit, the cheapest you can find, the wine that leaves you waking with a steel band around your head, thinking it's time to be a suicide case, the day has come. But they didn't have any of that here, and my, is wine expensive. Three bottles of the cheapest red. That's where we'll start, at least. Hopefully, you're a drunkard."

"I do enjoy my libations." I nod.

"You do enjoy your *libations*?" he mocks. "You don't sound like a drunk. I much prefer the company of drunks. Alcohol is the answer to surviving life, you know."

The waitress appears, a pretty blonde named Clara. She has one bottle of a California cabernet.

"I asked for three bottles," Hank says.

"Yes," she says. "Did you want me to bring them out all right now?"

"Yes," he says, "that's why I ordered three bottles. If I wanted one bottle, I would have ordered one bottle. I'd like three bottles."

"I'd be happy to bring you your second bottle when you're ready for it," Clara says. She opens the cab and fills our glasses, each a quarter of the way full. As soon as she leaves, Hank picks up the cab and fills each of our glasses to the rim. He sets the empty bottle on the table. I'm afraid he's going to holler after the waitress that we're ready for our second bottle, but he lets it go.

"That's why I never liked places like these," he says. "They serve alcohol, but they don't like drunks. Where's the sense in that?"

"Well–"

"We could have met at the track, that would have been a good idea." He takes a drink. I follow suit. "I missed out on the tight blondes like her," he gestures to Clara's path, "at least when I was young. I was physically horrific to them, they didn't want anything to do with me." He touches his wine glass to his cheek, cratered with scars of acne. "Later, they started sniffing around, shacking up, always when there was something to take, they were there."

"And you resent that?"

"No. I was happy to give it to them. I made up for the lost time of my youth."

"Were you ever in love?"

"Yes, I was in love. I wrote *Women*. I was in love with the research that I did while writing *Women*." His face is a patchwork of heavy features, eyes that labor to stay open, a mouth trying not to smile.

"But I was in love, real love, but love and sex only came late for me. Sex came with success and love came late in life. Sex is good when you can't sleep, I didn't sleep nights. If you don't have a night shift at the post office, maybe you have a girl to pass the night with. Love is a fog that burns away with the first daylight of reality. It feels and gnaws and dissipates. I won't say I changed late in life, but things changed. Life changes, love changes, when the body starts to go. Where's that second bottle?" He looks around for Clara. "Listen, baby, love is a dog from hell."

Clara returns with a second bottle. She and Hank have silently agreed to tolerate one another, though all three of us know that she has the power to boot us at any time.

"Thank you, thank you," Hank says. She returns his smile and leaves. I fill our glasses again to the rim. My head hurts in anticipation of tomorrow.

"Without alcohol I would have committed suicide a long time ago," he says and raises a hand to smooth his gray hair, curling at the neck. "What is the point to work your shit job for misery day in and day out if you can't drink a pint of whiskey at the end of the day? Anyone would go crazy with an existence like that, anyone. But with alcohol you can keep going, you can move through life and you've got your hangovers to pay for but you survive them and then you're back and revived and you can muster through your shit job again to get to that pint of whiskey. Alcohol saves the poor bastards."

"What did you think of *Barfly* once they'd finished making the movie?" I ask.

"Let me ask you something, do I look like Mickey Rourke?"

"Let me ask you something," I counter, "have you seen Mickey Rourke lately?"

"How different could he be?" he asks.

I contemplate pulling out my iPhone to display then-and-now Mickey Rourke pictures, but Hank is off and running again.

DRINKING WITH DEAD DRUNKS

"I hate people and I'd like for them to stay as far away from me as possible. There's not a lot of truth in people and they want to take what they can from you, just like you, here, now, taking from me. Using me, that's what people do. That's what you all do."

"Don't get all worked up, old man," I say. "I don't need to see one of your tantrums."

We're silent for a moment and I wait for him to explode. The pause is weighted, but then he laughs. "Ha! I'll need more wine than this for you to see me at my finest."

We seem to be on safe territory and I'm thankfully drinking with a less volatile Bukowski than I'd expected. We're halfway through the second bottle. The cheapest red at The Library Bar is actually not that cheap. I'm buzzed.

"For someone who hates people and all that they take from you, you sure did offer yourself up to them a lot."

"I didn't offer myself to them, I did poetry readings and interviews, and there they always were with cameras and recorders. I gave them my soul and they took it, but I took their money. I can't really say who wins. It was all perfect; it was all a mistake. What does it matter." This is not a question.

"I like this wine," I say.

"Me, too."

"But tomorrow is going to be painful."

"It's just the hangover. Get through it, start again. On the morning of the worst hangover of my life I woke and looked up, feeling like I had a cleaved head. I looked out the window and saw a man fall. A human body, feet first, straight in a line, he had a tie on, neatly tied, and he fell in slow motion. Bodies don't fall fast."

"Jesus. What happened to him?"

"I don't know. I decided not to look out the window."

"That's horrific," I say.

"It's not that bad, at least not for me. I didn't jump off the building, though. *Childhood* was horrific. Childhood was horror with a capital 'H'."

THE MICKEY MOUSE CLUB

"You wrote about it in *Ham on Rye*," I say.

He nods. "*Ham on Rye* was harder to write than the others. It was harder."

"Did anything good come out of your childhood?" I ask.

"Well, being beaten by my father taught me how to type."

"How so?"

"When you get the shit kicked out of you long enough, you have a tendency to say what you really mean, you have all the pretense beaten out of you. In that respect, my father was a great literary teacher." He pauses and drinks. "My father taught me the meaning of pain, pain without reason."

Clara approaches with a third bottle. As she opens it, she studies us, deciding whether or not it's okay to give it to us. Both Hank and I sense this and adopt our best behaviors. I smile at her politely. Hank looks away, studies the book titles lining the shelves. She tops off each of our glasses and retreats.

Hank looks at me and we breathe a sigh of relief. "Close call!" he says. "I thought teacher-lady was going to give us what for."

"Me, too."

"What were we talking about?" he asks.

"Your father," I say. "I was just about to slit my wrists."

"Let's move to happier subjects."

"Mickey Mouse?"

"Mickey Mouse was a three-fingered son of a *bitch*," he hisses. "Mickey Mouse is the antithesis of anything true or real or living. Give me any kind of hell, baby, I'll take life as a depressed alcoholic on the street without a whore. I'll take anything over having to ever see another image of Mickey Mouse. Three-fingered son of a bitch."

"Really? I thought everyone liked Mickey Mouse?"

"No, you don't. You know exactly how I feel about Mickey Mouse and that's why you mentioned him."

He's right. I concede by refilling both of our glasses, which leaves a few ounces in the bottle. Hank takes it from my hand and drains it.

"You think that tight blonde will bring us a third bottle?" he asks.
"That *was* our third bottle."
"A fourth, then?"
"Chances are slim."
"Fine. Let's find a dive bar like we should have from the start."
"Okay, after we finish these." I raise my glass to his, regretting having filled it to the rim. I take a sip and sit back in the chair, sinking into comfortable leather. I'm drunk, so going to a dive bar is probably not a good idea. It's also a wonderful idea, and I know that I'll listen to the devil on my shoulder, not the angel. I let my eyes close for a second.

"I'm going to take a piss, kid." I feel Hank's hand on my shoulder. I open my eyes and look up at him. "I'll be right back," he says.

"Okay," I say, then let my eyes fall shut again, just for another moment.

"Ma'am."

I wake with a heavy head. I've drooled on myself. I sit up and wipe my chin with my sleeve.

"You'll need to pay your bill now." It's Clara, who clearly doesn't want me to remain there, passed out and drooling.

"Yeah, okay," I say. I fish a credit card out of my purse and look around. Hank is gone. The glasses are empty. A cocktail napkin sits before me. The first things I see are the unmistakable Mickey Mouse ears. It's a doodle with artistic promise. Then I look at the rest of the drawing and see that Mickey is displaying oversized genitalia. It's signed H. C. Bukowski. I think about putting the drawing in my purse, then imagine explaining this version of Mickey to my children.

I quickly turn the drawing face down as Clara returns with my card, then walks away. I leave her a moderate tip for her tolerance, as well as Hank's drawing, because I think he would want her to have it.

JACK LONDON
WHEN THE FAVORITE HAUNT IS HAUNTED

BY ELAINE AMBROSE

I'm in Oakland, California – just a corkscrew's throw from Wine Country – yet I'm heading to Heinold's First and Last Chance Saloon, a rustic bar that dates back to 1880. I doubt that their wine list is included in *Wine Spectator*, but that's tolerable because I'll find a wine bar later, right after I interview Jack London.

The Saloon resembles the faded image in the old photographs from 132 years ago and not much has changed. The original building was constructed out of wood salvaged from an old whaling ship, and the weathered boards are held together by rusty nails and layers of paint. The place earned the name First and Last Chance Saloon because it was where sailors, fishermen, and travelers quenched their thirst before or after a journey at sea. A large sign perched on stilts above the building boldly announces the pub's claim to fame: Jack London's Rendezvous.

I walk in and notice old gas lights still in use, walls covered with historical photos, a working potbellied stove, and a floor that slants because of damage caused during the great earthquake of 1906. The pub is full of salty locals and curious tourists. I sit at a table beneath a hand-scrawled sign "Reserved for Jack London," and a bartender wearing a perky bow tie and period clothing saunters over.

"I'll have a Jack and Coke," I say, in deference to Mr. London.

DRINKING WITH DEAD DRUNKS

"And, can that be a Diet Coke?"

"Coming right up," the bartender disappears behind the huge, tilted bar. He brings the drink just as Jack London comes in the door and makes his way to the table.

"Bottle of Jack Daniels and a glass," he says as he sits down. George delivers. London nods his head in appreciation.

"This is my favorite saloon," he says while pouring a drink. "I wrote *The Sea Wolf* at this very table. Now they say it's haunted, but I've never seen any ghosts. Well, not when I was sober!"

We make polite introductions, touch our glasses, and enjoy a drink. I'm impressed with his youthful looks and then remember that he died at age forty.

"You're such a prolific writer," I say with genuine awe. "In twenty years, you wrote twenty-one novels, twenty-five short stories, two memoirs, and forty-seven plays. That's amazing."

"Don't forget the essays," he adds. "And the short story collections."

"How were you motivated to write so much? What inspires you?" I'm extremely curious.

"As I wrote in *The Sea Wolf*, it is the nature of life to dream of immortality. Maybe that's all I wanted."

"Well, you're immortalized by the huge sign on the roof."

"So true," he laughs.

"Speaking of *The Sea Wolf*, Wolf Larsen is the name of the protagonist in that novel. Didn't you model the character after a man you met in this pub?"

"Yes." London nods. "That would be Alexander McLean, a nasty cur of a captain if there ever was one. But the mean ones make for the best characters. We drank in this very saloon, and I despised him so much that I made him immortal."

"But he doesn't have a sign on the roof!"

London nods and pours another drink as George the bartender brings me another Jack and Diet Coke. I feel a hand on my back and turn, but there's no one there. I decide to go easy on the drinks.

WHEN THE FAVORITE HAUNT IS HAUNTED

"One more thing about inspiration," he says. "Don't loaf and invite inspiration; light out after it with a club."

I make a mental note to dig into my files after I get home and pull out all the half-finished short stories and ideas for novels I intend to write some day. And I am determined to find the necessary club.

"I have not been afraid of life," he continues. "I have not shrunk from it. I have taken it for what it was at its own valuation. And I have not been ashamed of it. Just as it was, it was mine."

He swallows the drink and pours another. I wait for the next soliloquy and know I won't be disappointed.

"There is an ecstasy that marks the summit of life and comes to the artist, caught up and out of himself in a sheet of flame; it comes to the soldier, war-mad in a stricken field and refusing quarter; and it came to Buck, leading the pack, sounding the old wolf-cry, straining after the food that was alive and that fled swiftly before him through the moonlight."

"I remember another great quote from *The Call of the Wild*," I say, concentrating to get it correct. "Kill or be killed, eat or be eaten, was the law; and this mandate, down out of the depths of Time, he obeyed."

"Yes, you've read the book."

Just then an empty chair turns toward our table. We laugh it off and taste our whiskey.

"Tell me about your childhood. Wasn't your mother a spiritualist?"

"Yes, she claimed to channel the spirit of an Indian chief. I never saw the guy but I went along with it to impress my friends. I think my father was an astrologer, but we're not really sure. My birth certificate perished in the fires that followed the earthquake of 1906 so I don't know who was listed as my father. My mother married a guy named John London and that's how I got my last name."

"What was your motivation to travel to Alaska and be part of the Klondike Gold Rush?"

DRINKING WITH DEAD DRUNKS

"By age thirteen, I was working eighteen-hour days at a cannery near Oakland. All I dreamed about was going out to sea. Then I became a hobo and a part-time sailor and continued to visit this bar we're sitting in now. Johnny Heinold, the owner, loaned me money to attend the University of California in Berkeley. I spent time in this saloon and met characters for my future novels and short stories, but I wasn't making much money. Then my brother-in-law convinced me to sail to Alaska in search of our fortune. I was twenty-one. I returned as broke as ever, but I had a burning desire to write. In 1903, I sold *The Call of the Wild* to *The Saturday Evening Post* for $750 and the book rights to Macmillan for $2,000."

"That's equivalent to $75,000 in today's money."

"If you say so."

"Critics have compared the literary quality of *The Call of the Wild* to *Walden* and *Huckleberry Finn*," I say.

"Well, there are other critics who say I plagiarized some of my writing. I admit that I use incidents from newspaper clippings for some of my material, and I write stories that are similar to what has been written in other books. So, yes, I am guilty of copying other authors' timelines and situations for my own stories. So shoot me."

He laughs and pours another drink. I'm thinking about London's mother and her séance with an Indian chief as George brings me another drink and a basket of salted pretzels. We munch the snacks and I decide to not mention the Indian.

"I'll tell you a fact," he says. "I'd much rather write short stories than novels. You can write a powerful narrative in 7,500 words. Sometimes I feel that my novels are just great short stories stretched out to fill space for a bloated book. You have more flexibility and freedom with short stories. I've written with themes that include science fiction, sports, motorcycles, boxing, anthropology, the Hawaiian islands, and socialist politics. Books are much more confining."

He drains the bottle into his glass. Another crowd comes in from the nearby ferry port, and thirsty patrons belly up to the crooked bar. George works the room, slapping down coasters, working the taps,

WHEN THE FAVORITE HAUNT IS HAUNTED

and sliding cold beers across the tables. The room hums with energy and potential characters.

"Life provides all the raw materials you need to write about," London says. "Just look around for ideas for your next short stories. That guy in the fancy suit over there needs to be a corrupt business owner. And that man wearing the faded overalls is a hopeless worker, destined to work hard and die poor. The other one with the fisherman's boots, his luck is about to change."

As I look around the pub with London on this imaginary pursuit of ideas and possible plots, I notice a photograph of Johnny "J.M." Heinold – the man who purchased the pub in 1883. A chill goes down my back as I see one eye wink at me. Maybe London is correct. The place is haunted. Or, maybe it's because I've consumed the third Jack and Coke. I notice that London's bottle is empty and he's passed out on the table. Obviously our interview is over so I call a cab.

"Remember," he lifts his head and mutters to no one in particular. "Life is not always a matter of holding good cards, but sometimes, playing a poor hand well." He slumps back onto the table, and I walk across the crooked floor as the front door mysteriously opens. I take a breath of fresh air and leave the past behind.

DRINKING WITH DEAD DRUNKS

Edgar Allan Poe
The Humorist

By AK Turner

Edgar Allan Poe sits next to me, huddled down in his chair like a frightened child. We're only a minute into the previews and he's wincing with every image that flashes on the mammoth screen before us. This was a bad idea. I hand him one of three flasks filled with cognac, the stash hidden in my purse, hoping it will help. He accepts the flask, eyes still on the screen. In the light and dark of the movie theater, I see his profile perfectly. His nose is pointier than I imagined. Other than that, he's much the same. His hair turns him into a caricature of himself. The bags under the eyes are profound.

The movie is *The Raven* starring John Cusack. We're at the Landmark Theaters on President Street in Baltimore. Edgar turns to look at me. He's caught me staring at him.

"Is *that* supposed to be *me*?" he asks.

I look to the screen where Cusack displays creamy white skin, a perfect complexion, nary a spider vein to be found. In the scene, he's supposed to be drunk, but his eyes reveal a remarkable clarity.

"Well, yeah, sort of," I concede.

"His head is enormous!" says Edgar.

I'm not sure if he's talking about the size of John Cusack's head in real life or the size of John Cusack's head on a movie screen. Either way, he's right.

Just having been thrown out of a bar, the faux-Poe on the screen walks down a somber street. He drinks from a small glass bottle. He's angry. With an ounce or two of booze left, he throws the bottle to the street where it smashes. The real Poe and I look at each other, our expression an agreement of doubt. We both know that a true drunk would never smash a bottle before consuming every last drop.

"I thought this was a rendering of *The Raven*," says Poe.

"Well, it's more like someone imagining what it would be like if you were solving crimes based on some of the things that happen in your stories."

"Then why did they call it *The Raven*?" he asks.

"I guess that's what people associate most with you."

We watch the pendulum scene. It is grotesque, disgusting. Both Edgar and I wince at the exact moments the director intends. The movie is just getting started, but with silent agreement, we stand and leave. As we make our way out of the theater, images of the pendulum and its victim fresh in our minds, Edgar turns to me and says, "You know, I wrote a lot of humor, as well."

Outside we find sunshine. Poe and I each carry our flasks discreetly and from my shoulder hangs an oversized bag. There are flowers inside, for later, and I imagine they aren't faring too well. We walk along Thames through Fells Point.

"I spent a lot of time here," he says.

"Me, too."

"I used to drink at that bar," he gestures to The Horse You Came In On Saloon. "In fact, that was the last place I ever took a drink."

"I used to wait tables at a sushi joint somewhere around here," I say.

Edgar looks at me. "Impressive." His face is blank and dry, then explodes into an unexpected grin. I'm relieved. "Thanks for the cognac," he adds.

"You're welcome. I don't think I've ever had cognac before, but I like this."

THE HUMORIST

"We need it after what we just witnessed." He's still trying to shake the pendulum scene. "I guess it's still the macabre that everyone likes?"

"Yes, I'd say so."

"Interesting. I wrote in so many different forms, but that was always the draw, the macabre."

"You were quite the literary critic, too, right?"

"Yes, and I carry no regrets about any of it, particularly Longfellow."

"I wouldn't expect you to regret a thing."

"I was not critical of everything, only the writing that merited it. I have never had a tolerance of obscurity for obscurity's sake."

In the clink of a glass, the sky darkens and proceeds to rain upon us.

"Do you want to go see your old house on Amity?" I ask.

"Yes." He smiles. "Let's."

We catch a cab and take refuge from the rain in the backseat. The driver is pale, thin with severe features. He has an Eastern European look to him. He also looks quite similar to Edgar.

"Where to?" he asks, with an accent I silently guess to be Lithuanian.

"Give me just a second," I say, rooting around in my enormous purse for my notes. I pull out a torn scrap of paper and read the address. "We're headed to 203 Amity Street."

"I could have told you the address," whispers Poe.

"You mean the Poe house," the driver says.

"Yes," I nod. "And if you wouldn't mind, could you take Lombard instead of Route 40?"

"Happy to," the driver agrees.

"Determined for me to relive my final moments, are you?" Edgar asks.

"Oh, I'm sorry. Do you not want to drive along Lombard?"

"Just a jest, my dear," Poe reassures me. "I'd be happy to see Lombard Street again."

DRINKING WITH DEAD DRUNKS

The rain falls harder, sounding like fallen rocks on the roof of the cab. Lombard is behind us and we take the MLK Jr. Boulevard over to the Poe house on Amity. I pay the cab driver, whose eyes seem almost as sunken as Edgar's. As the cab departs, Edgar and I stretch in the welcome but unexpected return of sunshine. The sidewalks steam.

Poe's flask is empty. He holds it up to me. "Not very big, is it?"

"No," I frown, finishing the last of my own flask. "But I have more."

With another feeble attempt at discretion, I refill our flasks from the larger one within my bag.

"What else have you got in there?" he asks.

"It's for later."

"Oh, God. It's not a human heart, is it?" he asks.

"No," I promise with a laugh.

We pocket our refilled flasks and make our way to the door of the old brick building, only to find that it's closed.

"What a shame," I sigh.

A notice on the door explains limited hours as a result of decreased funding.

"It wasn't much to see, in any case," says Edgar. "No matter. As long as we have more to drink, there must be more to see. Where shall we journey next?"

"I do have one more stop in mind," I say.

"Wonderful. As long as you are not taking me to my own grave or such nonsense."

"Oh," I mutter.

Edgar rolls his eyes. "That is our last destination? You are taking me to see my own grave?"

"Well, I don't know, I thought it would be interesting."

"Why is everyone so consumed with death?" he asks.

"You're the one who wrote about all this stuff," I protest.

"Yes, but I wrote a lot of other works," he huffs.

We walk and drink, along the way we're offered weed, crack,

THE HUMORIST

and a few other things with which I'm unfamiliar, but that I can only assume also are illegal drugs.

"*Eureka* was my masterpiece," Edgar insists. "Did you ever read that?"

"Well, sort of," I say.

"What does that mean?" he asks.

"No," I change my answer. "I didn't read it." This is easier to admit than truth, which is that I *tried* to read it. "But don't worry, people remember you for work other than just the dark stuff. Many writers who came after you consider you a pioneer in terms of science fiction and detective fiction."

"Good," he says. We drink. My lips, mouth and throat feel simultaneously numb and on fire.

"And people remember other things about you, too," I say.

"Such as?"

"Your wife."

"Virginia."

"Yes, Virginia. She was your–"

"Truest love?" he attempts to finish my sentence.

"I was going to say 'cousin'."

"Well, that hardly matters."

"And she was thirteen when you married."

"And taken too soon," he says. "She was very dear to me."

I decide not to press on the issue of marrying his thirteen-year-old cousin, because it's obvious that those things were not important at all. I feel the need to change the subject.

"Tell me about Rufus Griswold," I request. "He was kind of an ass, wasn't he?"

"One of many," Edgar agrees. "I had many enemies and he was surely one of them. Don't ever believe a word from him about me. His only aim was to shred my character."

We're finding it difficult to walk and talk at the same time, periodically crashing into one another as drunks are prone to do. In an effort to counter our lack of balance, I loop my arm through his and we continue.

"Oh, my!" Edgar says. I look up and see that we're here, on the corner of Fayette and Greene. "Where are we?"

"This is the Westminster Hall and Burying Grounds."

"And this is my grave?" he asks. He's staring at his own name, there's no need for me to answer. "It's enormous!" he exclaims.

"Yep," I nod. "Just like John Cusack's head."

Edgar walks around the monument, surprised to find that his are not the only remains buried here. "And Virginia is here, too?" He looks at me for confirmation. I nod. "They must have moved her," he says. "She was buried in New York. She died there."

We sit on the edge of the grave and I bring the three red roses from my bag. They are more than a little damaged from the walk.

"You brought me flowers?" he asks.

"It's kind of a Baltimore tradition," I explain. "At least, on your birthday, someone brings three red roses and cognac to your grave." I don't add that the tradition has dwindled in recent years. I withdraw the third, larger flask from my bag as well. It's no longer full, having dipped into it back at the Amity house. He touches the petals of the roses, already wilting, and takes the flask from me.

"May I?" he asks, holding it up.

"Of course," I say. "Finish it. I'm drunk, in any case."

The weather turns, the sky darkening for only a moment before the rain begins to fall again.

"Let's get out of this rain," I say.

"Thank you," he says, "I'll stay."

We acknowledge one another in silent farewell before I walk crookedly in search of a cab, and with hope that no one else will offer me crack. At the end of the block I flag down a car. As I get in, I look back to see Edgar holding the flask in one hand and stroking the 'V' of Virginia with the other.

The taxi circles the block, giving me one last look at the grave. Poe is gone, though the flask and flowers remain.

Selected Works of Dead Drunk Writers

ERNEST HEMINGWAY
F. SCOTT FITZGERALD
TENNESSEE WILLIAMS
DYLAN THOMAS
HUNTER S. THOMPSON
JACK KEROUAC
RAYMOND CHANDLER
TRUMAN CAPOTE
JOHN CHEEVER
JAMES JOYCE
WILLIAM FAULKNER
FREDERICK EXLEY
O. HENRY
CHARLES BUKOWSKI
JACK LONDON
EDGAR ALLAN POE

ERNEST HEMINGWAY
1899 - 1961

In Our Time (1925)
The Sun Also Rises (1926)
Men Without Women (1927)
A Farewell to Arms (1929)
Death in the Afternoon (1932)
Winner Take Nothing (1933)
Green Hills of Africa (1935)
To Have and Have Not (1937)
The Fifth Column and the First Forty-Nine Stories (1938)
For Whom the Bell Tolls (1940)
Across the River and into the Trees (1950)
The Old Man and the Sea (1952)
Paris: A Moveable Feast (1964, posthumously)
Islands in the Stream (1970, posthumously)

F. Scott Fitzgerald
1896 – 1940

Novels
This Side of Paradise (1920)
The Beautiful and Damned (1922)
The Great Gatsby (1925)
Tender Is the Night (1934)
The Last Tycoon (1941, posthumously)

Short Story Collections
Flappers and Philosophers (1921)
Tales of the Jazz Age (1922)
All the Sad Young Men (1926)
Taps at Reveille (1935)

Tennessee Williams
1911 – 1983

The Glass Menagerie (1944)
A Streetcar Named Desire (1947)
Summer and Smoke (1948)
The Rose Tattoo (1951)
Camino Real (1953)
Cat on a Hot Tin Roof (1955)
Orpheus Descending (1957)
Suddenly, Last Summer (1958)
Sweet Bird of Youth (1959)
Period of Adjustment (1960)
The Night of the Iguana (1961)
The Eccentricities of a Nightingale (1962)
The Milk Train Doesn't Stop Here Anymore (1963)
The Mutilated (1965)
The Seven Descents of Myrtle (1968)
In the Bar of a Tokyo Hotel (1969)
Will Mr. Merriweather Return from Memphis? (1969)
Small Craft Warnings (1972)
The Two-Character Play (1973)
The Red Devil Battery Sign (1975)
Vieux Carré (1977)
A Lovely Sunday for Creve Coeur (1979)
Clothes for a Summer Hotel (1980)
The Notebook of Trigorin (1980)
Something Cloudy, Something Clear (1981)
A House Not Meant to Stand (1982)
In Masks Outrageous and Austere (1983)

Novels
The Roman Spring of Mrs. Stone (1950)
Moise and the World of Reason (1975)

DYLAN THOMAS
1914 – 1953

18 Poems (1934)
Twenty-Five Poems (1936)
The Map of Love (1939)
Portrait of the Artist as a Young Dog (1940)
New Poems (1943)
Deaths and Entrances (1946)
Twenty-Six Poems (1950)
In Country Sleep (1952)
Collected Poems (1934–1952)
Quite Early One Morning (1954, posthumously)

Drama

The Doctor and the Devils and Other Scripts (1953)
Under Milk Wood (1954, posthumously)

HUNTER S. THOMPSON
1937 – 2005

Hell's Angels (1966)
Fear and Loathing in Las Vegas (1971)
Fear and Loathing on the Campaign Trail (1972)
The Curse of Lono (1983)
The Rum Diary (1999)

JACK KEROUAC
1922 – 1969

The Sea Is My Brother (1942)
Orpheus Emerged (1945)
And the Hippos Were Boiled in Their Tanks, with William S. Burroughs (1945)
The Town and the City (1949)
On the Road (1957)
The Subterraneans (1958)
The Dharma Bums (1958)
Doctor Sax (1959)
Maggie Cassidy (1959)
Book of Dreams (1960)
Visions of Cody (1960)
Lonesome Traveler (1960)
Tristessa (1960)
Big Sur (1962)
Visions of Gerard (1963)
Desolation Angels (1965)
Satori in Paris (1965)
Vanity of Duluoz (1968)

Poetry
Book of Sketches (1952–1957)
Mexico City Blues (1959)
Book of Blues (1954–1961)
The Scripture of the Golden Eternity (1960)
Scattered Poems (1971, posthumously)
Pomes All Sizes (1992, posthumously)

RAYMOND CHANDLER
1888 – 1959

Novels
The Big Sleep (1939)
Farewell, My Lovely (1940)
The High Window (1942)
The Lady in the Lake (1943)
The Little Sister (1949)
Playback (1958)

Screenplays
Double Indemnity (1944)
The Blue Dahlia (1946)
Strangers on a Train (1950)

TRUMAN CAPOTE
1924 – 1984

Other Voices, Other Rooms (1948)
The Grass Harp (1951)
Breakfast at Tiffany's (1958)
In Cold Blood (1966)
Christmas Memory (1966)
Answered Prayers (1986, posthumously)

John Cheever
1912 – 1982

The Way Some People Live (1943)
The Enormous Radio and Other Stories (1953)
Stories (with Jean Stafford, Daniel Fuchs, and William Maxwell) *(1956)*
The Wapshot Chronicle (1957)
The Housebreaker of Shady Hill and Other Stories (1958)
Some People, Places and Things That Will Not Appear In My Next Novel (1961)
The Wapshot Scandal (1964)
The Brigadier and the Golf Widow (1964)
Bullet Park (1969)
The World of Apples (1973)
Falconer (1977)
The Stories of John Cheever (1978)
Oh What a Paradise It Seems (1982)

JAMES JOYCE
1882 - 1941

Chamber Music (1907)
Dubliners (1914)
A Portrait of the Artist as a Young Man (1916)
Exiles (1918)
Ulysses (1922)
Pomes Penyeach (1927)
Collected Poems (1936)
Finnegans Wake (1939)

WILLIAM FAULKNER
1897 - 1962

Soldiers' Pay (1926)
Mosquitoes (1927)
Sartoris (1929)
The Sound and the Fury (1929)
As I Lay Dying (1930)
Sanctuary (1931)
Light in August (1932)
Pylon (1935)
Absalom, Absalom! (1936)
The Unvanquished (1938)
The Wild Palms (1939)
The Hamlet (1940)
Go Down, Moses and Other Stories (1942)
Intruder in the Dust (1948)
Requiem for a Nun (1951)
A Fable (1954)
The Town (1957)
The Mansion (1959)
The Reivers (1962)

FREDERICK EXLEY
1929 – 1992

A Fan's Notes (1968)
Pages from a Cold Island (1975)
Last Notes from Home (1988)

O. Henry
(William Sydney Porter)
1862 - 1910

Novels
The Four Million (1903)
Cabbages and Kings (1904)
Roads of Destiny (1919)
Rolling Stones (1919)
The Gentle Grafter (1919)

Short Stories
"girl"
An Afternoon Miracle
Best-seller
A Blackjack Bargainer
Blind Man's Holiday
Buried Treasure
The Caballero's Way
The Cactus
A Call Loan
A Chaparral Christmas Gift
Calloway's Code
A Chaparral Prince
Christmas by Injunction
Confessions of a Humorist
Cupid a la Carte
The Detective Detector
The Dog and the Playlet
Georgia's Ruling
The Gift of the Magi
The Handbook of Hymen
He Also Serves

CHARLES BUKOWSKI
1920 – 1994

Notes of a Dirty Old Man (1969)
Post Office (1971)
Factotum (1975)
Women (1978)
Ham on Rye (1982)
Barfly (1984)
Hollywood (1989)
Pulp (1994)

Poetry

Flower, Fist, and Bestial Wail (1960)
Poems and Drawings (1962)
Longshot Poems for Broke Players (1962)
Run with the Hunted (1962)
It Catches My Heart in Its Hands (1963)
Crucifix in a Deathhand (1965)
Cold Dogs in the Courtyard (1965)
The Genius of the Crowd (1966)
2 by Bukowski (1967)
The Curtains Are Waving (1967)
At Terror Street and Agony Way (1968)
Poems Written Before Jumping out of an 8 Story Window (1968)
A Bukowski Sampler (1969)
The Days Run away Like Wild Horses over the Hills (1969)
Fire Station (1970)
Mockingbird Wish Me Luck (1972)
Me and Your Sometimes Love Poems (1972)
While the Music Played (1973)
Burning in Water, Drowning in Flame (1974)
Africa, Paris, Greece (1975)
Scarlet (1976)
Maybe Tomorrow (1977)

JACK LONDON
1876 – 1916

Novels
Cruise of the Dazzler (1902)
A Daughter of the Snows (1902)
The Call of the Wild (1903)
The Sea-Wolf (1904)
The Game (1905)
White Fang (1906)
Before Adam (1907)
The Iron Heel (1908)
Martin Eden (1909)
Burning Daylight (1910)
Adventure (1911)
The Scarlet Plague (1912)
A Son of the Sun (1912)
The Abysmal Brute (1913)
The Valley of the Moon (1913)
The Mutiny of the Elsinore (1914)
The Star Rover (1915)
The Little Lady of the Big House (1916)
Jerry of the Islands (1917, posthumously)
Michael, Brother of Jerry (1917, posthumously)

Short Story Collections
Son of the Wolf (1900)
Chris Farrington, Able Seaman (1901)
The God of His Fathers & Other Stories (1901)
Children of the Frost (1902)
The Faith of Men and Other Stories (1904)
Tales of the Fish Patrol (1906)

Edgar Allan Poe
1809 – 1849

Selected Works
Morella (1835)
Ligeia (1838)
The Fall of the House of Usher (1839)
The Murders in the Rue Morgue (1841)
A Descent into the Maelström (1841)
The Masque of the Red Death (1842)
The Pit and the Pendulum (1842)
The Gold-Bug (1843)
The Tell-Tale Heart (1843)
The Black Cat (1843)
The Premature Burial (1844)
The Purloined Letter (1844)
The Facts in the Case of M. Valdemar (1845)
The Imp of the Perverse (1845)
The Raven (1845)
The Cask of Amontillado (1846)
Hop-Frog (1849)

Drinking with Dead Writers **Series**

Drinking with Dead Women Writers
Drinking with Dead Drunks
Drinking with Dead Crooners (2013)

DRINKING WITH DEAD DRUNKS

ELAINE AMBROSE
AK TURNER

Mill Park Publishing
Eagle, Idaho
www.MillParkPublishing.com

Mill Park Publishing

Made in the USA
Charleston, SC
24 October 2012